Freedom Fences

Art & Nova

Blessing to you as you continue to minister to others who search for fences.

Marlene Ka[illegible]

Blessing to you both as you experience God's freedom. Thanks for pastoring Mel & Lois

Jerry

Freedom Fences

How to set limits that free you to enjoy your marriage and family

Gerald W. Kaufman
L. Marlene Kaufman
Anne Kaufman Weaver
Nina Kaufman Harnish

Herald
Press

Scottdale, Pennsylvania
Waterloo, Ontario

Library of Congress Cataloging-in-Publication Data

Freedom fences : how to set limits that free you to enjoy your marriage and family / Gerald W. Kaufman . . . [et. al.].

p. cm.

ISBN 0-8361-9125-0 (alk. paper)

1. Marriage. 2. Marriage—Religious aspects—Christianity. 3. Family. 4. Family—Religious aspects—Christianity. 5. Conduct of life. 6. Autonomy (Psychology). 7. Self-control. 8. Moral conditions. I. Kaufman, Gerald W., 1939- .

HQ734.F7475 1999

306.8—dc21 99-22114

The paper used in this publication is recycled and meets the minimum requirements of American National Standard for Information Sciences—Permanence of Paper for Printed Library Materials, ANSI Z39.48-1984.

Website for Herald Press: www.mph.org
Library of Congress Catalog Number: 99-22114
International Standard Book Number: 0-8361-9125-0
Printed in the United States of America
Book and Cover design by Jim Butti

06 05 04 03 02 01 00 99 10 9 8 7 6 5 4 3 2 1

We dedicate this book to all of the courageous people everywhere who choose to become free through contained living. Our great hope is that our children and grandchildren, Keri, Alyssa, Caleb, Ashley, Lara, Taylor, Adam, Seth, and others who may come, will live in a world of true freedom.

Table of Contents

Foreword

If it is true that "good fences make good neighbors," then perhaps we ought to be looking at the fences in our homes.

In this book Gerald and Marlene Kaufman and their two daughters, Anne and Nina describe the value of choosing limits, symbolized by fences, within marriage and family. The limits we set on sexuality, time, language, and responses to conflict are maintained best by our commitments to a higher purpose for our marriage—one that serves God, our churches, and our communities as well as ourselves and our family. Within a set of chosen boundaries, we ironically become free.

What kind of fence best serves the purpose of freedom? Imagine three kinds of fences—a wall, a picket fence, and a boxwood border.

Walls

Some families live behind a virtual Berlin Wall; sealed off completely from the outside world by a sense that evil is so powerful that children, especially, should not participate in the world at all. This type of family is the direct antithesis to the family that lives without any fences, completely exposed to the whatever images of sex and violence pervade the media, and open to all moral perspectives, which results in commitment to none.

Here at Goshen College in Goshen, Indiana, we

have a meditation garden made up of stones and rocks from around the world, mortared together into one wall. Gerald Kaufman, a member of our Board of Overseers for twelve years, contributed to this wall, dedicated in April 1997.

One of the "rocks" in the wall is actually a fragment of the Berlin Wall, made of exceptionally dense material. The student who gave this remnant of the Cold War commented on how difficult it was to break up the wall. Sledgehammers were not strong enough in many cases. And yet what joy it gave people to destroy that wall! For decades it seemed impervious to freedom. Its purpose was not to allow people inside to develop freedom but to keep the freedoms outside the wall unavailable. We have all known families who try to keep freedom outside the fence rather than inside it. Sometimes the children in such families relish the opportunity to break down such walls. They feel it was there to punish rather than to guide.

As I read this book, it seems to seek an alternative to both the Berlin Wall and no walls. In order to understand it, we have to think about alternative kinds of fences.

Picket Fences

Do the Kaufmans wish to return to an ideal American family of the 1950s—the "picket fence" family in which the roles for father and mother and children are predetermined and unchanging and in which freedom inside the walls is subdivided according to gender and age? I think they handle this question deftly. All kinds of families—traditional, two-career, blended, chosen—can benefit from their advice, and no one type is exalted over others. But the picket fence is too jagged and too impervious to represent the kind of fence the Kaufmans suggest for families.

Hedgerow Fence

The image that comes to my mind when I think of family fences is that of the boxwood shrubs that surrounded the backyard of our house on Eighth Street in Goshen, Indiana. They kept our children from playing on the extremely busy State Road 15 that bordered the yard on the west. They offered us privacy for picnics and ball games without walling us off from our neighbors. They were organic, which meant they could be trimmed down to the ground if they had been neglected and would grow out again. The whole family had to work at maintaining them. Even the children took their turns at the trimmer, the rake, and the wagon, carting off the pruned branches. When they got big enough, the children made a game of jumping over the fences, but they always came back home again. In so many ways, the hedge itself represents the kind of safe, permeable, organic nature of family life the Kaufmans recommend.

Robert Frost's poem "Mending Wall," which declares that "good fences make good neighbors," begins by saying, "Something there is that doesn't love a wall." The Kaufmans know this is true, and they offer us a world in which the benefits of separation are combined with the benefits of freedom. These are the fences all our families and we clearly need.

Shirley Hershey Showalter, president
Goshen College, Goshen, Indiana
March 19, 1999

Author's Preface

It is hard to know exactly how the idea for this book got started. It was given a boost two years ago when our pastor asked Marlene and me to preach a sermon on marriage. At first we were reluctant because after thirty-seven years of being counselors and thirty-eight years of marriage, we had grown a bit weary of speaking about the subject. At least in traditional ways.

We knew we had nothing new to offer about better ways to improve communication, resolving conflict, achieving sexual compatibility, and sharing the household chores. We believed that most people who would hear the sermon had already tried such suggestions as putting chocolate kisses under their spouse's pillow or leaving love notes in their brief case to improve their marriage. If we were to proclaim a sermon, it could not include those worn-out ideas, good as they may be.

We chose instead to talk about the difficulties of "surviving freedom in marriage." In a world with fewer boundaries for behavior, how are some marriages being destroyed by freedom? The idea received positive feedback from a number of people. They encouraged us to do more with it. Our denominational magazine, the *Gospel Herald,* published the sermon. Later, publisher Herald Press, accepted the idea for this book.

As counselors we have heard many stories from clients about their troubled marriages and problems in their families. Many came from people who were well educated and well informed about human behavior.

Somehow knowing what they should do was preventing them from making wrong choices. As counselors we are limited in our power to keep clients from having affairs, working too many hours, accepting destructive lifestyles, or making people into better parents.

Most people mean well. They do not intend to do wrong things. It is increasingly clear to us that the primary reason for marital and family imbalance reside in the culture. Morally our culture has lost its way. The ability to think critically about decisions is low in a culture that emphasizes that freedom matters more than responsibility. It is further compounded when it holds that the fruits of freedom are always edible and suggests that wrong choices have no consequences. In this void, is it any wonder people are losing their way?

If this book seems unpsychological in its approach, that is intentional. We believe that some of us in the mental health and counseling fields have at times contributed more to the problems of our culture than to finding solutions. Our professions have played a part in helping to create a generation that is more self-centered than other-centered; in finding a psychological rationale for offensive and harmful behavior; and in developing names and labels for new emotional ailments which supposedly can only then be resolved through therapy.

Undoubtedly, some of our approaches may be helpful to people who are in genuine despair, but in the larger picture they are somewhat like adding one more lifeboat to the *Titanic*. They are good for the few people they save, but they do little to solve the larger problem in our society.

We have also tried to keep this book untraditional by staying away from psychological clichés and the jargon of the profession. Forgive us when a few slip through. Generally this book is not built around client stories because we did not want to exploit them to make a point. Some stories in this volume are totally fictitious and do not come from any particular people. The final chapter (13) includes freedom stories from a variety of people who wanted to share important parts of their life with you.

This book is not a scientific treatise. While we quote from some authorities, we make no pretense to be experts ourselves on the subject of human behavior. Even as we cite sources, we do so with some hesitation because in this field today's big theories become tomorrow's dust collectors. The bibliography reflects a number of secular sources that share similar concerns about the changes in our society that affect our marriages and family life.

We are mainly social observers who have been permitted into the private lives of many people who are searching for direction in a world that has few road maps. We are also surveyors of the larger North American scene as we evaluate trends and movements. As Christians we look with more than passing interest at the direction of the church.

The surrounding culture has created tentativeness in leaders who understandably want to be inclusive and nonjudgmental. In this environment leaders often seem afraid to lead, teachers to teach, prophets to prophesy, and parents to parent.

The book is based upon the belief that freedom only has value when it has constraints. Not the constraints of autocracy, but the social and spiritual code that comes from community discernment under the guidance of the Holy Spirit. A code that assumes that none of us can be totally moral on our own.

On the morning walk Marlene and I take, we pass the elementary school. Signs along the street warn drivers to slow down to protect the children. Many do, although probably not at the recommended low speed. However, when the police car is parked by the school, all drivers observe the speed limit precisely. Within the human spirit is the tendency to exceed boundaries unless they are confronted by authority that has meaning, an authority with the power to create consequences.

We are not advocating returning to "the good old days." The past had plenty of flaws too. We are suggesting that, as a Christian community, we work together to create fences that have meaning for our day. We reject the cultural view of recent decades that said that to be free is to have and do whatever we want.

This book attempts to look at ways our marriages and our families can erect fences that provide true freedom. We recognize that we write this book from a white, middle-class perspective. That is our place in life and the community in which we live. We hope people in other communities can find the information helpful and adaptable in their own environment.

This book was written as a family project. Marlene served as the coordinator, technical director, and a cocreator of ideas. She kept us on task. And with the special privilege that comes from being a spouse, she was the chief critic to Gerald, the primary writer. It was a good way to test the strength of our marriage! She was especially effective at spotting my verbal excesses. If there are parts of the book that make sense, give the credit to her.

Our daughters, Anne and Nina, were also integrally involved in the creation of the book. They sat with us in planning meetings, did some of the writing, and critiqued every word written. They helped us understand that people nearly sixty years old and people around thirty sometimes see things differently. They helped us modify some of the writing so that it would speak to their generation.

Anne's husband, Todd, participated in planning meetings, played guitar to soothe our nerves, and contributed a personal story. Nina's husband, Craig, also took part in the planning meetings and was an energetic supporter of the project. His very helpful ideas became part of the text.

Our son Nate was the cyber expert who got all of the electronics running. He was on call day and night and even tried to rescue an entire chapter after I pushed the wrong button on the computer. Without his technical help, we might still be on chapter one. His wife, Cathy, kept cheering us on in hopes that the finished product would be helpful in the raising of their three young daughters.

Our son Brent and his wife, Cheryl, gave long-distance support from Goshen, Indiana, and were available to continue to teach us the real meaning of freedom. Their unconditional love is an ongoing inspiration. We thank the entire family for the sacrifices they made during the past year as their parents and grandparents have been, at times, preoccupied.

We also owe a debt to a panel of reviewers who coached us on our way. These include Diane I. Bleam, Macungie, Pa.; Glenn Brubacher, Leamington, Ont.; Ray Hurst, Harrisonburg, Va.; Rachel Miller Jacobs, Goshen, Ind.; Delphine E. Martin, Waterloo, Ont.; Joe Neufeld, Regina, Sask.; Carmen Schrock-Hurst, Pittsburgh, Pa.; and Jane Wilson, Champaign, Ill. They convinced us to cut down on our use of commas and kindly told us when things did not make sense.

One tried to be especially helpful on a chapter she had evaluated; she said it had good ideas but she doubted that it would win a Pulitzer prize. We revised that chapter! All comments were carefully considered and most were folded into the text. They were immensely helpful. Indeed it felt like the book was a group project which was made easier by the thoughts of many kind people.

And a special thanks to our editor, James E. Horsch, from Herald Press who gently guided us on the maiden voyage. He was there when we needed him but stayed out of the way as we moved through the process. We hope that in some small way our conjoint efforts will be rewarded through readers who will celebrate new freedoms that come from living within chosen boundaries.

Gerald W. Kaufman
September 12, 1998

1

Surviving Freedom Through Restraint

"You are free from the law, but that doesn't mean you are free to do wrong. Live as those who are free to do God's will at all times."
1 Peter 2:16 (TLB)

"Everything is permissible"—but not everything is beneficial. "Everything is permissible"—but not everything is constructive. Nobody should seek his own good, but the good of others.
1 Corinthians 10:23-24 (NIV)

A Story About Freedom Fences

A story is told of a young family who settled on the vast prairie of the western Kansas. Times were tough and the challenges many. Every family member needed to help out. The family was close and worked together as a unit. There were few outside intrusions into their way of life. They each made sacrifices for the benefit of everyone. For the family, life was good. They had each other. They were free.

Each of the children left home for college and eventually married. In time the parents had difficulty managing the cattle and working the fields alone. They sold their farm and moved into town. Some years later, the children felt nostalgic about their childhood and asked their parents to return with them to the "home place." They had many good memories of their life together on the prairie and wanted to reclaim something that was important from their past.

When they arrived at their childhood home, it was abandoned and run down. But upon seeing the homestead, old memories were revived. The family began reliving a piece of their life that had shaped them. As they were peering out over the large expanse of land, one of the daughters noticed a fence off in the distance. She had not remembered it from childhood. She pointed it out to the family. Her siblings had forgotten it as well.

The parents assured them that it was there when they were growing up. They knew because they had put it there. Now it seemed out of place. What purpose did it serve? Was it to keep the coyotes out or the cattle in? Was it a property line? No, the mother explained, we put it up for your protection while you were playing. We wanted to have it far enough away from the house to allow you freedom but close enough that we could still see you before you got lost.

The Universal Wish for Freedom

Freedom is a wonderful gift. People feel strongly about their freedom. It is a very emotional issue. Deep within the human spirit is the desire to be free from restraints. Most of us handle freedom well most of the time. We live responsible lives, enjoy the fruits of our hard work, and go about our lives unimpeded. We are respectful of the boundaries of other people and expect they will do the same for us. We read what we want, speak freely, worship the way we are comfortable, and make those decisions that we believe are best.

Stories of achieving freedom are common throughout history, even to the present day. When South Africans were overturning years of apartheid, they sang, "Freedom is coming, freedom is coming, oh, yes, I know, I know." Their cause had been spurred onward by the example of Martin Luther King Jr. in the United States several decades earlier. In his famous speech at the Lincoln Memorial in Washington, Dr. King recited lines from an African-American spiritual: "Free at last, free at last! Thank God Almighty, we are free at last! "

As the Cold War came to an end in the late 1980s, Berliners chanted freedom songs as the wall that divided their city came down. And even though they still do it tentatively, Northern Irelanders celebrate new freedoms that have eluded them for centuries. People want to be free from repression. From war. From prejudice. The human spirit cries out for freedom.

Celebrate New Ways of Being Free

But it is not just from invading armies, from repressive leaders, or from unjust social systems that people want to be freed. Wheelchair-bound quadriplegics are captives if they cannot leave their homes or get jobs. Many of them are now enjoying a fuller life because society is reshaping curbs so they can navigate their wheelchairs and providing elevators and ramps so they can enter public buildings. We are all more free by our interaction with people who are challenged in ways we are not. Being confronted with the needs of others who are different from ourselves expands our boundaries and makes us more complete people.

Women enjoy a new freedom that comes from being valued for their minds and their gifts. They are shedding the stereotypes that have demeaned them. Now most are comfortable with the idea that they are not the "weaker vessel." Opportunities that extend beyond their traditional roles continue to open up to them. A woman is more than a physical body and an object of sexual attention.

Men are also freed by new understandings of their role. No longer are the tough exterior and a sculpted physique necessary to feel adequate, although some may still believe that. Many husbands feel a freedom that comes from developing skills in the kitchen and as primary parents. Those who are in relationships of mutual respect with their wives feel an intimate freedom which men who insist on superiority can never feel. These husbands know that they can only be free if their wives are also free.

Marriage is experiencing freedom because of new and fuller understandings of sexuality. Not only are the discoveries about the differences and the similarities about the sexual response freeing, but the emotional and spiritual interpretations are helping spouses experience intimacy in new ways. Many are now able to see that sex is more than a physical act. They understand that intimacy inside the bedroom is an extension of the environment outside the bedroom.

Modern medicine has freed many people from disease. Surgery is less invasive. Testing is less traumatic. There is hope that cures are coming for the most threatening illnesses. Medications are being found to relieve the symptoms of many kinds of mental illness. These enable many people to live productively. New counseling techniques are being developed which help people come to practical solutions for their problems. Most do not need to go through years of endless searches for hypothetical causes. And there are more songs of freedom with many more to come. The freedom story will continue to be sung in new ways and with new themes. And each will celebrate the escape from captivity.

The Down Side of Freedom

Not all freedom songs have good endings. In some ways, the more freedom we have the more we are likely to abuse it. Having more freedom tends to make us want even more. It is in the excesses of freedom that we become captive to our own passions. Some people interpret their freedom to mean they have choices which are not limited by boundaries. They believe that what ultimately counts the most is their personal happiness.

The moral code has been changing in recent times, and individuals are left to figure out their own standards. In that vacuum, abuses of freedom ultimately leave people as captives of their own self-centeredness. But choosing wisely is the essence of freedom. Placing voluntary restraints on ourselves, valuing our own limitations, and respecting the dignity of others makes us free people. More joy comes through what we give up than through what we acquire, through sacrifice than through power. As a people who have been given more gifts of freedom than any previous generations, we are perhaps the least grateful.

Common Mistakes in Handling Freedom

The problem with freedom is that it allows us to make wrong choices. There have never been more choices available than there are now. Most choices have minor consequences. We are on more committees than we should be. We work slightly longer than we should and are late for dinner too often. Once in a while we watch a movie that is a waste of time or eat a banana split after we are already full. We borrow money to make a trip that we did not need to make. Maybe we live in a house that is too large or drive a car that costs too much. Perhaps we said something nasty about the pastor to someone else. The list is endless.

Nobody makes all of the right decisions all of the time. Often these mistakes are relatively benign. Maybe morally neutral. But they require critical thinking. Does our decision making show carelessness? Insensitivity to other people? Carelessness about our health? Many of us have made decisions we wish we could do over again. They were made impulsively and for the wrong reasons. But we survived and learned from the experience. Most of us do not make the same mistakes repeatedly.

Major Mistakes of Freedom

For some people, freedom carries much more risk. They find it difficult to contain their choices. They keep stretching the boundaries until something or someone stops them. They are like a teenage boy I once knew when I worked at a home for delinquent boys. He had just been admitted to our home after he threw a brick through the windshield of a car. The car was parked directly in front of a police cruiser. He was promptly arrested and sent to our institution.

Later, when he reflected on the incident, he admitted he wanted to be caught. To be restrained. Freedom was too much for him to handle. He was much more comfortable within the structure of our institution. And he was not alone. Prisons today are bursting at the seams with people who cannot handle freedom. Drug and alcohol treatment centers are filled with people who cannot stop themselves from using substances which are addicting.

In his book, *Terry,* former senator George McGovern tells how his daughter died at the age of forty-five from alcoholism. Ironically, she died shortly before she was going to be admitted to a long-term secure facility. Perhaps structured living for an extended time would have saved her life. All of the Alcoholics Anonymous meetings, hospitals, detox centers, and counseling she had received had not been enough. In spite of the temporary good they might have done, these treatment programs had to give her the right to make choices when she walked out the door. Maybe she would never have been able to manage her life on her own, but it is clear that when she died, freedom without boundaries was dangerous.

In that same way freedom allows people to discard marriages because of addiction to the romance of affairs or because of sexual compulsions that cannot be contained within marriage. It is also freedom that permits individuals to work sixty hours per week, neglect marriage, or neglect even their own health. Some people refer to this as "workaholism."

Some people are obsessed with the success of their children. They push them for grades or for achievements in sports, in theater, or in music. The children become victims of the parents' desires. Many people interpret freedom to mean they can do anything they want without thinking about the consequences. They often believe that negative things will never happen to them. Mishandled freedom always has consequences. Some of them are tragic.

How Did We Get to Where We Are

If we can believe the evening news, society, marriage, and family life are in trouble these days. The stories of failure are discouraging. The statistics recited by the experts do not offer much hope. As society has become more relaxed in its standards for behavior, it would appear that some people are not able to think critically about their choices. While most people would say that the changes have brought many benefits, many do not recognize some of the insidious aspects of the new freedom. People often do not realize the mistakes they have made until the consequences are unavoidable. We have gotten into some regrettable habits that are hard to break because most of them feel so good. We may even be able to justify them to ourselves.

Living in a world in which secure boundaries are increasingly rejected, it is easy to believe that the real enemy of freedom is restraint as well as the people who try to restrain us. We live in a world of very strange contradictions. It angrily punishes some transgressors and then uses their stories to entertain us in movies and on stage. The line between heroes and villains has never been less clear. It is that same inconsistency that tells a twenty-year-old not to drink but defends fraternity drunkenness as a rite of passage. Morality is so fluid. So situational. Maybe it has always been like that. But if it is worse now, the following three reasons may have played a part:

1. Youth Found a Voice in the Protest Movement

What began as a protest over the Vietnam War in the late 1960s ultimately became a defining movement against authority and the moral code. Young people did not want to be drafted to fight for what many of them considered an unjustified cause. They were living during a time of great expectations because of the space race, advances in technology, and many other changes that impacted a rapidly growing youth culture. This spirit of optimism was severely jeopardized by the leaders of a country who were sending them off to a battle that many of them did not want to join.

These young voices of protest eventually were effective in stopping the war. They had come to distrust the authority of most older adults. At first they were angry at politicians. Then it spread to parents, business owners, people in academic life, and the police. No longer would those in power have the ability to make unilateral decisions. This generation of youth was demanding participation. In many sectors of society, authority has never been the same since. "Historical events produce nodes of unease that can forever shape the attitudes of young people coming of age at that time"(Kagan, *Family Therapy Networker,* Sept.-Oct. 1998, p. 62). Dr. Kagan believes that massive social changes like the antiwar movement influence the values of individuals for the rest of their lives.

Once the "king" was deposed, the moral code was also up for grabs. The rules which governed social and religious behavior for generations were challenged. The rock music festival at Woodstock was an enormous symbol for the new moral code. "Free sex," nudity, drugs, and alcohol were given legitimacy by the legions who were there and by the untold numbers who were not. It was as if within a short period of time, the forbidden had become common. Parents and other moral custodians could only sit by this torrent of change and watch. Many railed against what was happening, but no one could stop it.

Over the years, authority has tried to regain its seat. Backlash movements have sprung up from time to time against crime, abortion, welfare, and similar single-issue symptoms of the abandoned code. While all have had various degrees of success, leadership will never be the same. In many places it is tentative. Leaders step forward only after the pollsters have done their work. Decisions are not made without the input of focus groups. Consensus has replaced conviction. Within the church, being prophetic is permissible only with a two-thirds majority vote.

The new moral code continues to be in flux. No one is quite sure where to put fences. Some are embarrassed by the excessive legalisms of the past carried out by some leaders who appeared to be arbitrary. Today a spirit of tolerance and acceptance is in. Judgmentalism is out. In this time of uncertainty, people are reluctant to define boundaries.

2. The Commercialization of Protest

While the generation of protest was bringing down authority and traditional morality, business and the media were not far behind. The spirit of protest became fertile ground for new products and new markets. Entertainment that stretched the boundaries developed big audiences. New displays of sexuality sold well on Broadway, in the movies, and in many magazines. While television continued to operate within some constraints from the government, it constantly stretched the limits. Products of self-gratification were good for the bottom line. Doing what brought pleasure became a right.

While people in the mainstream of society may not have endorsed most of the expressions of protest, they were still influenced by the spirit of the times. Their lifestyles became less "buttoned down." Their views of sex and its expression were expanded. They read with interest the discoveries of sexual researchers like Masters and Johnson and bought books about new techniques. They became more risk taking and questioned the standards which were learned from their parents and their church.

In the years since then, the "new morality" has become commonplace. People have become numbed to profanity, vulgarity, and incivility. Lifestyles are only the concern of the people practicing them. With computers becoming a part of many households, few people are publicly questioning the hours children and their parents are spending on them. There is not enough talk about the dangers of the chat rooms and the new levels of voyeurism that computers make possible. Self-centeredness keeps developing new outlets.

Some churches have become apologists for the abandonment of standards. Grace has replaced guilt in the standard lexicon. Many have not addressed the consequences of the new moral freedom. Some try by developing support groups for divorced people or having programs for blended families. But many are uncertain about what to do about subjects like sexual unions that occur outside of marriage. Speaking out about lifestyle has become tentative. It has become more proper and correct to address issues of justice. The distinction between the road which leads to life and the road that leads to destruction, which Jesus talked about in Matthew 7, has become less clear.

These changes in values have become pervasive, reaching the remotest parts of society. They are expressed from the fishing villages in Newfoundland to the Amish communities scattered throughout North America. Stories from both of these peoples tell of struggles with being affected by the dominant culture. The fishing families of Newfoundland lost some of their connection to the community ethos when television came to the Island. Instead of visiting in each other's homes and maintaining historical traditions, they became captive to television. Their new values began to be shaped many miles and cultures away. So it was with the Amish whose young people were increasingly exposed to ideas from outside their community. They wanted to drive cars, dress like other people, and have the symbols of freedom they saw all around them.

3. The Counseling Professions and Freedom

During the past three decades, there was a rapid growth in the counseling professions. Their leaders began to produce best-selling books. They appeared on the talk shows of radio and television. When there was a crisis in a community, their opinions were sought for how to deal with the fallout. They became the new chaplains to help people deal with trauma. Psychology became a hot topic. Its language became the core of some social conversations. Businesses used psychological concepts to help employees get along better, to increase productivity, and for marketing purposes. In some areas, money was allocated for programs intended to improve the self-esteem of children. Sensitivity groups and support groups were formed for virtually every affliction.

For the past three decades, the counseling professions have contributed to having vast numbers of people become self-focused and analytical of human behavior. Many lay people became "armchair psychologists." Labels and categories were created for a wide range of behaviors and personalities. People were encouraged to discover emotions that were supposedly hidden deep in the unconscious mind.

There is little doubt that this expansion of attention to human need has been of benefit to many people. Some with depression are now well. Some with anxieties or with poor self-images now live productive lives because of counseling. There is little doubt that society is more understanding and feels more compassion for human suffering because of this emphasis.

However, the benefits are not without unintended side effects. Some have become perpetual clients who keep looking for solutions for problems that need to be solved in other ways. Their primary focus in life is on themselves. Somehow the solutions offered through counseling are never enough. Some people are now labeled co-dependent, victims, or victimizers who can only get "well" when they follow the standard program for "recovery."

Some people interpreted the psychological theories to mean that being whole was to not be "hung up" by restraints. Being free meant setting their own standards or doing their "own thing" with little consideration for others. Some counselors participated in this process by encouraging their clients to question their childhood belief systems. They were openly disparaging of religious expression that they considered harmful to their clients.

Accepting Restraints

In the beginning of this chapter, the words of the apostles Peter and Paul gave guidance about freedom and restraint. Peter said we may be free from the law but we are not free to do wrong. We are only free to do God's will. Paul clarifies that because Christ came to give freedom from the law, this freedom does not mean everything we do is beneficial or constructive. Freedom means doing what is for the good of others.

Many people believe we have moved away from the type of legalism that Peter and Paul were talking about. Away from dress codes, bans on most kinds of entertainment, dietary requirements like avoiding red meat on Friday, and a variety of other practices that were common in the various branches of Christianity. While changes may have been overdue in the specific areas of life, the spirit of the times has spilled over into major elements of lifestyle.

We began doing things that were not in God's will,

that were not beneficial and constructive. These separated us from God and did harm to other people. When a people moves away from restraint, the potential for doing harm is unlimited. While most of us avoid the big failures, many of us brush up closely enough to be at risk. Fences on freedom are vital. Absolute freedom is neither possible nor wise. It is disorder, chaos. The issue is not whether fences are needed. Instead we ask which fences, where should we place them, and who should put them up?

When we choose to live within boundaries, we feel the comfort of knowing we are in God's will. The joy of being present with God cannot be compared with the temporary pleasures that can be found outside the fence. Living within the boundaries gives us the security that comes through making mature choices. Thus when we become adults we "put away childish ways." (1 Corinthians 13:11). We know that our choices will not bring harm and that through living within boundaries we bring happiness to others; in so doing we experience joy ourselves. The fences we choose bring freedom because they unite us with God and with the people we love.

Restraints Allow for Harmony

Stories of restraint take place all around us. One story came as an epiphany to me while my granddaughter was helping me play some tunes on our Autoharp. My belief about this instrument is that it sounds better when the chord keys are pressed before strumming the strings. That makes chords like I am used to hearing. They are pleasant and soothing. However, at the age of three, our granddaughter had other ideas. She thought that the music sounded better when all the strings were played at once. She wanted the freedom to hear all of the sounds, and I wanted the restraint that brought harmony. After a few minutes of each of us trying to convince the other of our point of view, we decided to move on to another activity and resolve that issue later.

Restrictions make recognizable, pleasing sounds on the Autoharp. In a similar way when a family is in dissonance, someone needs to press the chord key to change the cacophony into harmony. Someone needs to manage the household schedule better, to choose quality entertainment, to cooperate on family responsibilities, and to keep the promises that have been made to each other. In so doing, we discover true freedom.

Fence Building

Can we accept the belief that restraint is the friend of freedom? The old system of rule making was often arbitrary then, and it would be arbitrary now. Leaders in the past were frequently too isolated from the followers. Decisions about practice were made from the top down. As with the members of the early church, everyone today needs to contribute to decisions about how the new covenant is to be lived out. It is where "two or three of you are gathered in my name" (Matthew 18:20) that God is among the followers creating epiphany.

Among God's people, a theology of lifestyle is always a work in progress. It is an emerging system of boundaries based upon biblical interpretation and upon the realities of the day. This theology allows for a community of grace in which failure is understood and forgiven, a community in which appropriate guilt is a treasured gift.

We cannot be totally free to decide everything for ourselves, as if there were not any consequences to our choices. We do not drive on the side of the highway that suits us best, go to work just on days we prefer, or pay the amount of taxes we want to pay. None of us are free to annex our neighbors' property to give us a bigger yard or flaunt our wealth without a reaction from those who are poor. We cannot even be unfaithful to our marriage commitments without being criticized by most people.

The human condition calls for structure. We need reminders of the limits of freedom in order to make freedom meaningful. While some people may need more reminders than others, fences are for the protection of everyone. They must be erected to help us be people who live beneficial and constructive lives. The fences should be far enough from us to give us room to roam, but not so far that we get lost. Freedom is a wonderful gift. It is also an important responsibility.

In our families we need to be islands of contained freedom in a sea of uncertainty. Places in which children are comforted by knowing that parents are committed to each other and see the love of parents expressed during high and low times. We need to see homes where sacrificial love is the defining spirit. Where parents are comfortable with setting reasonable structures for their own lives as well as for the children's. We need an environment in which discovery happens because the time and space is secure and where joy springs from achievements which have eternal importance.

In our journey together through this book, we want to search for freedom fences that are relevant to your life. Obviously fences may be at different places for different people. But it is in dialogue with each other that we can discover true freedom as a community of grace.

Questions

1. When you hear the word "freedom," what does it mean to you?
2. When you hear the word "restraint," what does it mean to you?
3. As you reflect on your childhood, place your parents' lifestyle on the continuum.
   Total freedom — Complete restraint
   1 2 3 4 5
4. As you evaluate your current lifestyle, where would you place yourself?
   Total freedom — Complete restraint
   1 2 3 4 5
5. Give examples of current situations where you have been benefited by some of the new freedoms. Also describe where it has been helpful to have some fences.
6. From your perspective, what are the strengths and weaknesses of strong authority?
7. From your perspective, what are the strengths and weaknesses of self-direction?
8. How have the changes in the values and moral standards in our society affected the choices that you make?

Activity

Make a list of the freedoms you enjoy. Then make a list of the restraints that are imposed on you by yourself or by others. What do these lists tell you about yourself? Which list is longer? What, if any, changes are needed?

Bibliography

Covey, Stephen R.
1997 *The 7 Habits of Highly Effective Families*. New York: Golden Books.

Kagan, Jerome
1998 "How We Become Who We Are" in *Family Therapy Networker*. September-October.

McGovern, George.
1996 *Terry: My Daughter's Life-and-Death Struggle with Alcoholism*. New York: Villand Books.

Pipher, Mary
1996 *The Shelter of Each Other*. New York: Putnam Books.

Walsh, David
1995 *Selling Out America's Children*. Minneapolis: Fairview Press.

Whitehead, Barbara DeFoe
1996 *The Divorce Culture*. New York: Alfred A. Knopf.

Wink, Walter
1992 *Engaging the Powers*. Minneapolis: Fortress Press.

2

Freedom: Eden and Beyond

> You may eat any fruit in the garden except fruit from the Tree of Conscience—for its fruit will open your eyes to make you aware of right and wrong. Genesis 2:16 (TLB)

> For you were called to freedom, brothers and sisters; only do not use your freedom as an opportunity for self-indulgence. Galatians 5:13 (NRSV)

The Garden of Eden

God wanted to create a being who could make choices. A being who reflected God's image. As wonderful as the rest of creation was, it was without a soul. It did not have a reasoning, deciding being. Adam and Eve were a necessity. As a loving, caring Parent, God gave them an invitation to freedom, but it was accompanied by a warning: the choices of freedom will have consequences.

Thus it was in the creating of choice making that God originated conscience, that feeling in the soul that would serve as a guide for decisions. The kind of shame that comes from being naked. That feels a knot in the stomach when a wrong is done. A feeling of guilt that interferes with sleep.

In the midst of all of the physical beauty of the creation, God saved the best for last. The high point of the plan was experienced through Adam and Eve and their ability to choose to love God. But the Divine Parent did not just drop them off in the garden and wish them luck. God gave them freedom instructions: "You can eat from any tree except that one, and if you choose wrongly, there will be consequences" (Genesis 2:16). Freedom, but with limits. Boundaries that gave freedom meaning.

Parents sometimes know what God may have felt like in the garden of Eden. It is frightening to give children freedom. That first time parents hand over the car keys to their teen they, too, give instructions. They know their teen has reached an important stage of independence, but parents feel remiss if they do not also give some advice about how fast to drive. Or to make sure the teen obeys all stop signs and pays attention to the road. They explain why it is important to be home by 11:00 p.m.

God must be there in the background, nodding while the instructions are being given. Maybe even smiling. Freedom is wonderful and frightening at the same time. It is for God and it is for parents as well.

The Giving of the Law

The Ten Commandments (Exodus 20) were given to the children of Israel through Moses to help them maintain their relationships with God and with each other.

The first four Commandments were to serve as reminders to the people of the sacredness of their relationship with God. That the relationship should not be compromised by worshiping other gods and idols through profanity or forgetting the Sabbath. God knew that the relationship with humankind was in jeopardy if they lost their focus and if their loyalty was placed elsewhere. From the beginning God's people have always been engaged in an ambivalent relationship with their Creator. They have struggled with giving the total commitment that this relationship requires. However when people fail to do so they inevitably become secular.

The last six Commandments were given to govern relationships between people. A kind of civil code that gave instructions on how to treat each other. Violations of these Commandments would lead to destruction within the human family. God knew that people would not always be able to stop themselves and would need clear limits. However, God did not create structure as an end in itself or as an arrogant show of authority. After all, God was talking about murder, stealing, and adultery as well as other things that are vital to civility.

God never intended that the Law itself should be worshiped. It was only meant as a way to help the Israelites stay faithful to their Creator and respectful to each other.

The problem came when people began interpreting the Law and doing their own rule making. Sometimes the scribes and Pharisees even said they were doing it for God. Often leaders had their own interpretations of what God was saying. As God's law was being formed into the sacred canon, it became difficult to know what was from God and what was from people.

The Law became very intricate, if not obsessive. The smallest details of daily living were spelled out with great care. Details like what to do when wayward oxen gored other animals. Or how to deal with mold in their houses. There were so many instructions that people did not even have to think for themselves.

The Law became so complex that scholars had to interpret it for the people. Quarrels were common among leaders, causing factions. God's attempt to give helpful structure had become institutionalized. It was written down, it was interpreted, and it was kept on file.

Jesus Transforms the Boundaries

The Messiah came as the fulfillment of the Law and to deliver a new covenant. Jesus was very critical of the institutionalized Law and challenged the hypocrisy of many of its practitioners. Some of the people who defended the law were often more concerned with maintaining its purity than their relationship with the Creator of the Law.

Jesus brought a new order of life that was based more on the sacredness of relationships than on a written document. When asked his opinion about the greatest law, he replied, "You shall love the Lord your God with all your heart, and with all your soul, and with all your mind. . . . You shall love your neighbor as yourself" (Mark 12:30-31, NRSV).

Jesus spoke of changing lifestyle, of discipleship, and of sacrifice. He talked about the last being first and of giving up earthly life to obtain eternal life. These ideas were not emphasized in the canon. The teachings of Jesus threatened the defenders of the Law. His radical ideas made him a pariah among the people. They led to his death.

However, it is unfair to blame the defenders of the Law totally for their negative reaction to Jesus. They were simply following their belief that law is necessary for social order and for helping to maintain reverence for God. They took their obsession with the Law to levels that perhaps did more harm than good. They knew as God also knew that if people are ungoverned they are out of control. Unfortunately, the defenders often placed obedience to the Law above love.

Early Church Searches for Freedom

The early followers of Jesus were excited about the new freedom from the Law. Their Spirit-led enthusiasm was contagious and spread rapidly throughout the growing Mediterranean communities. Jews and Gentiles, men and women, slaves and free, rich and poor were now worshiping together. What a powerful breakthrough! The risen Christ must have had many opportunities to smile about followers using their freedom to spread God's love.

But old patterns are hard to break. In Galatians 5:13-15, Paul is faced with a group of believers who are arguing about the relevance of the Law in light of Christ's coming. Paul reassures them that they are called to freedom and not legalism, but says they should be careful not to become self-indulgent. They are to love and serve one another. If they do not care for one another, they will destroy one another.

Paul and the early church seemed to struggle with meshing the theological and the practical. Yes, you are free in Christ. No, you may not hurt yourself or God's people. In a way Paul appeared contradictory. How can you be free and yet have restrictions? If Paul's position sounds familiar, it is probably because it was similar to the instructions God gave to Adam and Eve "You are free, but . . . " Paul offered suggestions that he believed were appropriate for that time, place, and people. He created fences for faith and practice.

Modern Church Searches for Freedom

Through the centuries God has not changed. In many respects neither have people. People want to be free. Many times we use our freedom to serve God, but at times we mishandle freedom. It is an old theme with new applications. God told Adam and Eve that picking fruit from the Tree of Conscience would make them struggle continuously with choice making (Genesis 2:16-17, TLB). God was right. Humankind remains caught in that tension and thus still needs the guidance of the new covenant.

In recent times many people have chosen to live with fewer restrictions, but that has not made them freer. When people experience more freedom, made possible through the advances of modern technology and knowledge, some assume that moral and spiritual boundaries are not necessary anymore. Just because we have more technical knowledge does not mean we have more authority to write our own code of ethics. We too are called to freedom that is based on love and service, and not on self-indulgence.

Some People Manage Choices Well

Some people are quite good at governing their lives and take the teachings of Jesus seriously. Their list of sins is short. They love God, are in tune with God's Spirit, and love God's people. Their covenant is internalized, and they need few reminders. They have the ability to make good judgments about their behavior and are seldom swayed by shallow fads and movements. When the bandwagon comes by, they usually decline a ride. They make the tough choices well. Contained freedom is their lifestyle.

It is hard to know what they would have done in the garden of Eden, but they certainly appear to be good gardeners now. They tend to be the older brother in the prodigal son story (Luke 15). They have no particular inclination to rebel or to resist authority. They often have a hard time understanding why people break the covenant. They are comforted by the covenant, and it serves their needs. They are ethically mature.

Some People Need More Help with Managing Choices

Many people need extra help to manage their choices. The apostle Paul said he sinned daily and complained about his thorn in the flesh. He warned the Corinthians to not be complacent about the danger of falling into sin (1 Corinthians 10). He told them that no temptation was irresistible. Peter had his share of trouble, and we know about the choices Judas made. Making unloving choices is common in the human family. But is it more common to some people than to others?

Many people would lay the blame at the feet of Satan. It is said that Martin Luther believed so strongly in a personal devil that he threw his inkwell at him. In the Anabaptist tradition, Menno Simons talked about the kingdoms of good and of evil. As Christ is the Prince of the peaceable kingdom, Satan is the prince of the kingdom of darkness.

Over the centuries, there has been a persistence in the belief that a strong evil force exists in opposition to God. Many people believe that a struggle for the soul of humankind has always been waged between the forces of good and evil.

Some people believe that the evil force resides in individuals. They refer to it as demon possession. Indeed, Jesus cast out demons from a number of persons. It is hard to know what to make of this idea today. Our judgment can be so subjective. We think we can see demons in people we do not like or in people we do not understand. Sometimes the person believed by others to be demon possessed instead has a mental illness that can be treated with medication. It is difficult to discern clearly, and it is easy to make misjudgments.

Many people believe that others who perpetrate large-scale violence are under the influence of a sinister force. There are people who have suggested that evil is broader and resides in corrupt institutions. Walter Wink in *Engaging the Powers* regards the evil being as the "impersonal spiritual realities at the center of institutional life." Some refer to a feeling of darkness that hung over Hitler's Germany. Others see evil in racism, classism, and sexism. Regardless of how this question is answered, many people believe in this force personified by Satan. It is certainly a part of the biblical story.

Vulnerabilities Make Boundaries Imperative

That still does not answer the question about why people handle their freedom so differently. All of us encounter the same temptations, but our reactions vary greatly. Even people who are generally self-managed can have their moments of weaknesses and become destabilized by stress or trauma. Others make mistakes when they are struggling with chronic illness or have experienced a significant loss. Some are not as loving when they are hungry or short on sleep.

Strangely, there are some who fail when they are at the height of success. Weaknesses or the euphoria of success would appear to make people more likely to make poor choices. For them, while external structures are especially vital, their internal covenant may not be enough to keep them from doing harm.

Genetic Influences

From studies of identical twins, it appears that some of our choice making is influenced by genetics. Some studies suggest that as much as 50 percent of our personality is inherited. The most convincing evidence of this is seen in identical twins who were separated soon after birth and raised in different homes. Long-term follow-up evaluations of such twins have found a high degree of similarity in personality, choice making, and overall adjustment. If one twin had a lot of trouble, so did the other. If one made a good life adjustment, the other twin often did, too.

If we inherit other physical characteristics like body build and color of hair from our parents, it only seems logical that behavior, which originates in a physical, brain is also influenced by genetics. For certain kinds of conditions, scientists can even identify a specific gene that explains the condition. If this is true, it suggests that our freedom is affected by physical factors beyond our control. However, even geneticists would say that most people still have some choice in their behavior.

Biochemical Influences

There is also increasing evidence that our biochemistry, particularly in our brain, helps to determine how we feel and how we act. For example, in recent years much progress was made in understanding how the neurotransmitter serotonin impacts our personality. It is believed that when this hormone is improperly utilized by the brain, individuals become depressed, irritable, obsessive, and can have a number of other conditions.

Other brain and neurological conditions contribute to certain behaviors. Currently, there is much attention given to attention deficit hyperactivity disorder (ADHD) and attention deficit disorder (ADD). Formerly, some difficult children were labeled "strong willed." Today many of these children are believed to have a biochemical imbalance or some other brain irregularity.

Among adults who show signs of instability, there is increased understanding that physical factors affect their choices. People, for example, who have frequent job changes or cannot stay in relationships may not just be people who are selfish, arrogant, or irresponsible. Their choices may be influenced by factors within their bodies. If true, it raises ethical questions about responsibility for wrongdoing.

Family Influences

Our ability to handle freedom is taught in our families. Just as we learn to speak from our parents and siblings, we learn ways of thinking from them. How our parents handle freedom will influence the way we will handle our freedom. Parents tend to shape our worldview. We are molded by the discussions around the dinner table and on the trips taken together in the family van.

Many theories have been offered about the ways families influence children. Some blame parents for the problems of their children. While some of these ideas may be overstated, it is clear families do shape us. While the influence from our genes cannot be overlooked, there is little doubt that a good amount comes from what we learn.

For example, if we are raised in a family that has a lot of conflict, we tend to think that conflict is the norm until we visit a family that is peaceful. Surprisingly, even when we are exposed to other styles of conflict, we tend to repeat the patterns we know best. But God invites us to change the patterns even when we learned them in a family with unhealthy patterns. We are called instead to be imitators of Christ.

Learning Critical Thinking

If we are to handle freedom well, we need to learn to be critical thinkers who evaluate information before making choices. We will look at all of the facts available and decide if our choice will be beneficial or destructive and necessary or superfluous. To do well in today's world, all of us need to have analytical minds. Allowing ourselves to be drawn into harmful patterns by peer pressure is an escape from taking responsibility.

It is easy to understand why teens would be vulnerable to peer pressure, but it is much harder to understand that same behavior in adults. Some people make their decisions by default. By avoiding decision making, outcomes are often decided for them.

We live in an era in which critical thinking appears to be in short supply. Perhaps it is because we are surrounded by affluence or we live next to many people whose lives seem too easy. We accept the attitude of the secular world: do not worry, be happy, and do not think about your choices. This same world also encourages us to be open-minded and to avoid being judgmental. These influences from the surrounding culture persuade some people to set aside critical thinking.

Previous generations had difficult dilemmas to face. Many pacifists chose to not enter military service during wartime. Some even refused to work in industries that supported the military effort. Other Christians would not do commerce on the Sabbath. They thought to do so would offend God and keep storekeepers away from worship.

But today the sin list has become shorter and, perhaps with it, our ability to make critical decisions is weaker. Could it be that critical thinking is like a muscle that atrophies when it is not used? Might we be sacrificing some of our freedom through the lack of critical thinking?

For our nurture and guidance, God places us in families and in communities of faith. Knowing that some people will have a harder time than others, God expects the stronger to offer support to the weaker members.

The weak, with encouragement, can become strong.

However, the strong can become weak through the choices they make. They, too, need to be lifted up. Even though God does not want us to fail, the natural consequences of our wrong choices cannot be prevented. When that happens God continues to call us back to a life of love and restraint.

Freedom Fences

The God of the Ten Commandments and of the new covenant calls us to freedom through limits. God knows that free people live within boundaries. As Christians we need to discern together where those boundaries are to be placed today. These limits need to be far enough away to allow exploring and close enough to keep us from getting lost. Some of the fences on freedom could include:

1. Internalize a covenant of beliefs based on a close relationship with God and a belief that if we separate from God we alienate ourselves from our Creator and sustainer.

2. As a part of our commitment to God, we will be active members of a worshiping community to strengthen our faith as well as to receive instruction and encouragement from each other.

3. We covenant to live in an environment of health: individually, with our spouses, our children, and our community.

4. As a church community we will work together under God's guidance to develop a covenant based on eternal truth and applied to the unique

moments of today. It expresses both discipline and grace.

5. We will accept that there are natural consequences for all choices. If we continuously engage in high-risk behavior, we cannot expect to be spared from its effects. While forgiveness can restore relationships with God and with other people, it may not undo all of the consequences of poor choice making.

6. We will believe that true freedom is only experienced in an environment of chosen containment.

Questions

1. Do you believe God made the right decision by giving us a conscience and free will? Why?
2. How do you think the Israelites felt when they received the Ten Commandments?
3. How would you react if a current religious leader gave ten new rules from God? What would they be?
4. In the time of Jesus, in what way was he radical and in what way was he conservative? In what ways is his message radical and conservative today?
5. In the early church, there were disagreements about when to be free and when to set limits. Name several examples. What are the examples of our day?
6. If someone audited your choice making over the past year, would they find:
    a. The choices you have made are consistent

with your Christian values?

b. There is irregularity in your choice making but there is a general pattern to live out a Christlike life.

c. There does not seem to be any connection to your Christian walk and daily talk.

7. As you read the sections titled "Genetic Influences," "Biochemical Influences," and "Family Influences," are there any vulnerabilities you can identify in yourself or among your family members? If so, what are they and what can you do about them?

Activity

Write ten new commandments that would create fences needed for today's society.

Bibliography

Bridges, Wagner
1991 "Early Childhood and Its Effects" in *The Harvard Mental Health Letter*. V 8-2, p. 4.

Dowling, Colette
1993 *You Mean I Don't Have to Feel This Way?* New York: Bantam Books.

Keirsey, David, and Marilyn Bates
1984 *Please Understand Me*. Del Mar: Prometheus Nemesis Book Co.

Marlin, Emily
1989 *Genograms*. Chicago: Contemporary Books

Schwartz, Jeffrey M.
1996 *Brain Lock*. New York: HarperCollins Publishing Co.

3

Permanence in Marriage

Therefore what God has joined together, let no one separate. Matthew 19:6 (NRSV)

You shall love the Lord your God with all your heart, and with all your soul, and with all your mind, and with all your strength. Deuteronomy 6:5 (NIV)

Permanence in a World of Change

Never in the history of the human family has change come so rapidly. The senior generation has seen technology advance from the horse and buggy to flights to the moon. Telegraph machines have been replaced with cell phones that are capable of communicating from the remotest points on earth, whether with climbers on Mt. Everest or scientists at the South Pole. With such rapid change comes a mindset that expects obsolescence. The computer used to write the copy for this book is already out of date.

We have come to believe that nothing is forever. It is what some would call the throwaway society. Perhaps it is this spirit of change that has caused society to discard major pieces of the social fabric. For many people, the social and moral code is obsolete, and the standards that have shaped society for generations are no longer relevant to them. Parts of society have rejected fences while looking for freedom.

Discarding Marriage

With these changes some people see marriage as a temporary arrangement which can be nullified if a spouse does not meet all the needs of the other or becomes difficult to live with. Some of the wedding vows created by couples today hint at an escape clause. They emphasize that marriage is primarily for the happiness of each other and at the same time suggest that no spouse can meet all of the needs of the other spouse.

This approach says, "A truly 'healthy' marriage is one in which neither spouse gives up prerogatives or freedoms." (Whitehead, *The Divorce Culture,* p. 193). Care is given not to promise more than can be delivered. Little is mentioned about sacrifice, the importance of living with imperfection, or the importance of permanent covenant. It seems promises do not mean as much as they used to for some people.

Perhaps in part because of these changes, record numbers of couples today are divorcing. Studies have found that 67 percent of recent marriages end in divorce. (Gottman, *Why Marriages Succeed or Fail,* p. 16) Certainly, some divorces are necessary for the mental health and physical safety of one or both spouses. These divorces often occur in marriages in which partners are either unwilling or unable to change. But many marriages are discarded too quickly.

Just as my computer can be replaced by a better one, some people have the illusion that a new model spouse will be better than the old one. That flies in the face of the facts that show that second marriages have an even greater rate of failure than first marriages. But in this culture we have become increasingly intolerant of what we do not like. We are driven by the North American spirit of optimism that says that something better is just around the corner.

The Importance of Permanence

Can something as important as marriage be swept aside easily and not have consequences? Are there some things that never go out of date? In spite of all of the shortcomings of marriage, it is still an institution that is at the core of society. It is not something that has outlived its usefulness or is to be taken casually. Permanence in marriage is important at a number of levels.

To God

Permanence in marriage is important because it matters to God. God is a God of order who depends on promises being kept in all aspects of life. From the beginning, God entered into covenant with humankind intending that the promises would help people govern their choices. God sent Jesus in part to humanize the covenant and to give a living form to the promised covenant.

While Jesus freed people from the rigid practice of the law, which was common at that time, he did not replace promise. He warned that no one (or nothing) should be permitted to cause the marital covenant to be broken. All relationships are built around covenant; whether between God and people or between people themselves.

God knew from the beginning that promise keeping would be tough and gave us the advice in Deuteronomy to put our heart, soul, mind, and strength into keeping the covenant. A partial commitment does not work. Only a total commitment will make covenant succeed.

To the Church

Permanence is vital to God's family, the church. The church as a covenanted community depends on mutual trust. It holds common beliefs that create a bond. From this bond, people nurture each other and feel safe to engage in active dialogue, discernment, and even disagreement. People who break the covenant can find restoration in a forgiving community. This human family, with all of its failures, is still a place for homecoming. But it is in part the safety of covenant that brings people back together.

In contrast to secular organizations, the church draws its strength from a God of permanence. The marriage covenant is vital to the life of the church. The health of the family unit is central to the health of the church family. When one marriage fails, the entire church family suffers. Church friendships are divided. Loyalties are tested.

Sometimes in the choosing of sides between the divorcing spouses, the unity of the church is diminished. Because the church is made up of imperfect people in imperfect marriages, covenant is important to the church family as a fence that creates an environment of freedom.

To Spouses

Permanence is central to what makes marriage work. Some people seem to enter marriage unwilling to unpack their suitcases. They want to keep one foot outside the door. Marriage needs to be total and permanent. Anything less than that leaves the marriage partial, tentative, and at high risk for failure.

True intimacy will only ever be experienced in a relationship that has a permanent commitment. Other relationships may be more erotic or romantic but not intimate. Marriage can only work if there is trust. When trust is lacking, spouses are wary and doubting. Sometimes jealous. Only the security of permanence can take that away.

Trust is built around unconditional love that reaches out to the spouse in both the high and low moments. Marriage endures the stresses that come from illness, financial problems, or job disappointments. Promising faithfulness also tends to have a maturing influence. It is a human impulse to run when things get tough or even boring. Commitment to permanence requires spouses to be fully responsible adults. There are no escape clauses from adultness.

Permanence is the only protector of the sacred history of the couple and the best assurance of an undivided future for the family. It helps protect memories stored in the photo albums as well as giving the hope of family experiences that are yet to come.

Sadly, as increasing numbers of couples encounter brokeness, many of them lose significant things from the past and can only anticipate a compromised future. They lose the freedom that can come from sharing with a partner for a lifetime. A journey of two souls who celebrate the joys of both the high moments and the common. When looking back at a life together, couples can reap the benefits of keeping their covenant. They feel secure because of permanence.

To Children

Permanence is vital to the children. A child's view of the world and of self is given a healthy positive shape by a dependable bond between a mother and father. It is through the unbroken relationship with parents that children develop the ability to trust. It frees them to explore with confidence, experience joy, learn, and be forgiven when they step outside the boundaries. It is by living with both parents that children see adults working to solve problems and experiencing the joys that come from permanence.

Many adults who as children experienced divorce struggle constantly with low self-esteem, mistrust, fear of commitment, and sexual problems. (Berman, *Adult Children of Divorce Speak Out*, p. 31) Studies have shown that people who were part of their parents' divorce when they were young are at higher risk for divorce themselves.

Divorce is unsettling, and the effects can last a lifetime. While some things can be done to soften the impact, nothing can be done to remove all of the effects. Some divorced parents do a remarkable job of minimizing the losses for the children under very difficult circumstances, but as creative as they may be, they cannot totally eliminate the impact.

To Society

Permanence is critical to the health of society. Stable families, as well as singles who live responsibly, make up the core of a well functioning society. Even to the secular world, the marriage covenant is important. Society depends on the stability of monogamous marriage that stands in bold contrast to the instability that comes from promiscuity, cohabitation, and divorce.

The venereal diseases, cervical cancer, and AIDS that can come from sexual license are the legacy of a world without boundaries. The emotionally impacted children and the wounded partners of divorce carry their burdens into the broader community. The costs are social, financial, and spiritual.

Barbara Defoe Whitehead's book *The Divorce Culture* states that when divorce became more common during the 1960s, society ignored the negative impact. Instead various leaders suggested that divorce itself was only harmful if people handled it badly. They believed that the divorce experience made some children more self-confident.

Whitehead and others now question the assumptions that were emerging from the "divorce culture" because they saw evidence that the impact was not benign. When promises are not made or when they are made and not kept, society edges toward disorder. Keeping promises is essential for keeping social order. That is why God makes such a big deal out of it. It is necessary to the integrity of our relationships with God and our relationships with each other.

Common Struggles with Permanence

Sexual

Under the best of circumstances, many people find it hard to remain faithful to their spouses. In a sense it is unnatural to limit sexual curiosity and involvement in other relationships. There is both a biological and an emotional desire to connect with many people. It takes a conscious decision to stay within the boundaries of the marriage. Some people may be somewhat like children who are less interested in the toy they have than the one the other child has. They are driven by curiosity and by a need to possess what they do not have.

For men that drive is often based more on sexual passion, while for women the drive comes more from a wish to be in a relationship that is emotionally satisfying. These are powerful forces. They have always been a challenge for couples. Such dynamics become even more significant when the marriage is weak or under stress.

To keep marriage strong, men may need to deepen their relational skills and women may need to expand their understanding of male sexuality. The wonderful mystery of marriage is that men and women, starting at very different places, can learn from each other what intimacy really means.

Friendship Needs

No spouse can meet all of the friendship and social needs of the other spouse. It is common for both husbands and wives to maintain close ties with friends. Friendships are important. They provide new energy and fresh ideas. They can give personal validation that in some ways spouses cannot give. When friends are wisely chosen, they will be supportive of the marriage. They will be known by the other spouse.

However, friendships present a risk when they become more primary than the marriage. Cross-gender friendships are especially hazardous because of their potential for romantic and sexual involvement. These friendships can simulate the marital relationship when they include personal disclosures, humor, and other aspects that promote closeness.

The important consideration in any friendship outside of marriage is whether is has appropriate boundaries and whether it strengthens the marriage or detracts from it. When friendships are used to escape an unhappy marriage or to satisfy one spouse's unmet needs, they almost always contribute to the deterioration of the marriage.

Usually counseling is helpful for spouses to regain their perspective and fix what is wrong with the marriage. Friends and family can offer support during difficult times. However, their role may need to be limited because they are unable to see the big picture. Some even contribute to the conflict. Pastors and counselors can be more skilled and objective in their approach.

Personality Differences

During courtship, people are charmed and attracted to each other by their differences. Because of that, married couples are often quite different from each other. During the marriage, the charm is lost in day-to-day living. It is then that couples try to change each other. It rarely works! Partners can only change themselves.

Behaviors like leaving shoes in the middle of the floor or interrupting conversations can change. It only requires willingness on the part of the offender. However, some characteristics like being disorderly, intense, or perfectionistic are more deeply ingrained. While these characteristics may have looked different during courtship, spouses may need to learn to live with these differences. They are unlikely to change.

Routine

Marriage can become monotonous. It is a daily journey of ordinary people doing routine things. There is not much excitement in that. The menus served in the dining room start to taste the same. Conversations become unstimulating and repetitious. Spouses' bodies may no longer win contests. Sex can be unimaginative and programmatic. Even the house and the neighborhood can become tiresome. When monotony arrives, it is easy to be misled to believe that the marriage is deficient. However, life itself can be tedious.

Stresses

There are distractions that come from children, the pressures of jobs, and financial worries. They all draw down our energy and our spirit. It is hard to be on top of our marital game when we are always playing with a handicap. Spouses run dry. The occasional night out without the children may not be enough. There are still diapers to change, jobs to go back to, or bills to pay.

The problem with marriage is that is has to be lived in the real world. That is what makes the night out with the buddies look like so much fun or an affair so appealing. These distractions are not the real world and would suffer the same fate if they became ordinary.

Culture

To make matters worse society denigrates permanence in marriage through its entertainment outlets and its public figures. Marriage has become the butt of jokes. Famous people who have had multiple partners both within and outside marriage are rewarded with wealth and fame. Their lifestyles intrigue people.

We are indeed living in a culture of divorce in which monogamy is becoming the exception rather than the rule. It is easy for common people with common problems to believe that staying married is not important. Some of them are influenced by the dominant culture.

Uncommon Struggles in Marriage

Mental Illness

Sometimes the problems in marriage come from various mental illnesses and personality disorders. Because marriage depends so much on successful communication, mutuality, and the ability to form an intimate bond, it is difficult to meet the needs of both partners if one is not well.

Depression may be the most common illness that affects marriage. It is thought that in the general population, approximately 15 percent of people are depressed at some time in their lives. That may explain why some marriages fail. While new medications have been successful in restoring most people to health, some resist treatment and their spouses suffer with the results. Depressed people often have low energy and can be argumentative. Because they are not able to meet their own needs, they can give little to a mate.

Some people have a milder form of depression that is difficult to detect. They may not have the usual symptoms that would take them to doctors but their illness makes them difficult partners to live with. They may be restless and resist closeness. They often do not like to take responsibility. Not knowing the real source of their problems, they frequently blame their spouses for their unhappiness. They can generate severe conflict and then blame the spouses for becoming angry. When they withdraw they cannot understand why the spouses are unwilling to give them more "space."

These individuals often pursue solutions outside the marriage that cause further trouble. Sometimes it is relatively benign like taking night classes at local colleges or joining theater groups. Often it is higher in risk like going to nightclubs with friends or having affairs.

Other mental illnesses like obsessive-compulsive disorder, anxiety and panic disorder, schizophrenia, and a variety of other personality disorders also take a toll on marriage. In recent years some new discoveries about attention deficit disorder in adults are clarifying why some people who are disorganized or impulsive and who procrastinate have trouble in marriage.

These illnesses account for many of the divorces. Sometimes it is the spouse who is ill who terminates the marriage. Sometimes it is the mate who cannot tolerate the condition any longer, especially if the ill spouse resists treatment and is unwilling to accept the reality of the condition. Many people turn away from the very help that could preserve their marriage. Often they carry their condition into additional marriages. What a tragedy if the marriage is discarded because of the unwillingness to take a medication or to get professional.

Trauma from the Past

Some people enter marriage as wounded survivors of past experiences. Maybe their childhood was filled with conflict. Perhaps their parents divorced. Or they were never blessed and loved as they should have been. Some never found their places in a peer group. They were shy or excluded for reasons that they could not control. Some were abused physically, verbally, or sexually.

For others their pain may come from failures in romance during their adolescence or young adult years. They were rejected and now find it hard to trust. These make intimacy in marriage more difficult. They tend to select spouses who are themselves lacking in confidence or are abusive. It is very hard for wounded people to marry well or to be happily married.

Marriage never works well as therapy or to heal wounds. It never fills the cup that seems to have no bottom. Ironically it is often wounded people who marry impulsively and without considering the circumstances. The decision sometimes is made in anger and to retaliate against those who have caused the wounds.

It is important for people who were traumatized in the past to get professional help before they marry and to continue that help for a number of years into the marriage. Woundedness tends to generate more woundedness.

Trauma from the Present

Traumatic events during marriage can place a very heavy burden on couples. They can destabilize even healthy marriages. The serious illness of a spouse, child, or close family member can be difficult to handle. A child who is born with or acquires a handicap takes emotional and physical energy. The death of a child always draws heavily on the resources of a couple. These traumas divert from marriage the energy, communication, and love which is its lifeblood.

They frequently leave couples in grief. Often angry. Sometimes in despair. When the pain is not faced, couples tend to withdraw from each other. Their marriage is often a secondary casualty. It is important for couples to seek the support of others, including people who have gone through similar experiences. Their pastor can help them reconnect with the God of healing.

As more couples are postponing pregnancy into their middle and late thirties, many are faced with infertility. When couples want to have a child and are not able to, the effect on marriage can be significant. Not only is the couple's future changed by the inability to have children but issues of blame arise as well. A form of grief is almost always present.

If the couple seeks treatment, they may endure months of expensive and intrusive procedures that tend to make their sexual relationship more a medical experiment than a romantic experience. A couple who is unable to conceive may be disillusioned and discouraged. Couples who work through the failure can emerge with positive attitudes. Some people have trouble moving past their disappointments.

High-Risk Marriages

Because we are a people of covenant, it is hard to know when it may be necessary to end a marriage. Some people give up too quickly. With counseling, perhaps with medication, and with God's healing touch, many could have stayed together and become intimate partners. We are all diminished by unnecessary divorces. A sacred unit has been dissolved and there is never complete recovery.

But some people are too unstable to remain married. They are not well suited for the demands of an intimate relationship. Marriage will not make them well or heal their woundedness. It may make their problems worse. We may all want them to be healed, and it is appropriate to pray for a miracle. However, the demands of marriage can be beyond their abilities. Although medication and counseling can be helpful, many reject treatment.

Some people may not be able to be helped. Their woundedness is profound and pervasive. They can be very difficult, if not even dangerous, to live with. Their instability can tie up a congregation in conflict. Pastors and friends often do not know how to help them. Divorce may be the only solution for the spouse and for the children. The church needs to take a proactive role in helping couples resolve this most difficult problem. Creative approaches need to be found for the spouse who is unstable and for the spouse and children who have had to endure suffering.

Celebrating Commitment in Marriage

For most people, marriage is a union of two imperfect people who experience life more fully because of what each brings to the other. The number of couples reaching their golden wedding anniversary is increasing. Most say they would do it all over again with the same spouse in spite of the imperfections. There is something very civilizing about keeping commitments. Relationships have meaning only when spouses stand by each other during good times and bad. The real heroes of society are its members who are faithful to covenants and who can be counted on to honor promises.

Many married people love their mates. They laugh together, discuss the morning news at the breakfast table, worry together when their child is sick, discover new things with each other on vacation, disagree about the same things, are irritated by idiosyncrasies, worship together, find new ways of being intimate, and more. No human experience can consistently be richer and have more meaning. God had a special purpose in creating marriage. It is with gratitude that we meet each day with the spouses we have chosen. Covenanted marriage is a celebration of freedom.

A Freedom Story

A couple in their senior years had raised their family, sold their home, and moved to a retirement home.

Several years passed, and they enjoyed being together in their new apartment. They received frequent visits from their family and friends. Gradually the wife's health began to decline, and her eyesight weakened until she became blind. This made it necessary for the couple to move to a part of the home where the wife could receive more care. Her husband remained at her side.

He thought he could make the time pass more quickly by describing the happenings of the day. Many hours were spent relating the activities outside the window, in the courtyard, and in the play ground across the street. He welcomed the morning sun and the colors of the changing seasons. He was excited one spring to discover a robin building a nest on the window ledge. In great detail, he told his wife when the eggs were hatched, how the robins brought food to the chicks, and when they left the nest to fly on their own. It brought pleasure to her.

One day, shortly after the last robin flew away, her husband became ill and died a few days later. She was filled with sadness. She missed her husband in a number of ways. Including his stories of what was happening outside their window. One day the staff told her that a woman would be sharing the room with her. She waited several days for her roommate to get settled before asking her if she could tell the stories of life outside their window as her husband had done.

When the roommate heard the request, she was puzzled. There was a bit of silence before she answered, "Didn't you know that there isn't a window in our room?" When the roommate realized the importance of what had happened between this husband and wife, she said, "What a wonderful gift your husband gave to you. You must have had a wonderful marriage."

Permanence in marriage happens between people who express their love for each other through giving unselfishly. Who celebrate together even with constraints. It is within the fences that they experience the highest marital freedom. And the greatest degree of personal fulfillment.

Freedom Fences

1. Pastors will require intense premarital counseling and will be forthright with couples when they see potential negative patterns. Parents and friends can be helpful in the process of helping couples see themselves more clearly.

2. The average wedding and honeymoon today costs $17,000. Because those dollars have not improved the success rates for marriage, the couple could cut the cost of their wedding in half and use the savings for an annual marital checkup, counseling, and time away as a couple to enrich the marriage. This money could make a good start on a down payment for a house!

3. No job will ever be more important than marriage. That may mean limiting the hours at work, the amount of energy given to work, and the effect of the workplace culture on the marriage.

4. Friends will not be more primary than the marital relationship. Male and female relationships outside of marriage will not take on the characteristics of a marriage relationship.

5. Spouses will "leave" their families of origin

and "cleave" to each other. The extended families will be important in a supportive way, but they will not interfere with the primacy of the marriage bond.

6. We will reject the influence of the secular society on marriage by turning away from entertainment that degrades marriage and will actively challenge the view that divorce is an acceptable alternative for problems that could be resolved.

7. We will avoid the belief that happiness is found in material possessions or in external pleasures. True intimacy is found in the simple joys of life.

8. Marriage will not be based on artificial and unrealistic standards of romance and communication. We will celebrate both the ordinary and the moments of ecstasy, knowing that only within a trusting and permanent covenant can true ecstasy and intimacy occur.

9. If something in my background or in my health creates marital conflict I will take the necessary steps to correct it.

10. A spirit of mutual sacrifice will permeate the relationship.

Questions

1. Why is it so important to keep marital promises?
2. Who is affected when marital promises are broken? In what ways?

3. How can family and friends be helpful when they have serious concerns about someone's marriage? How would their involvement limit the freedom of the couple?
4. We can have meaningful relationships with many people. In what ways can those relationships be a threat to marriage?
5. Marriage is the association of separate individuals with their separate needs. How much can spouses be expected to give up for the sake of the relationship?
6. Why should other people care if I get a divorce, especially if it feels so right to me?
7. When is it appropriate to discuss my marriage problems with other people?
8. Who should help monitor these marriage fences?

Activity

1. How will these six areas be affected by the permanence and health of your marriage? How would these six areas be affected by the deterioration of your marriage?

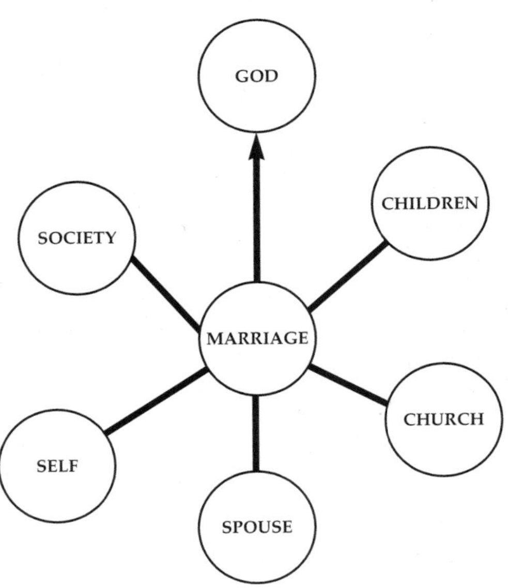

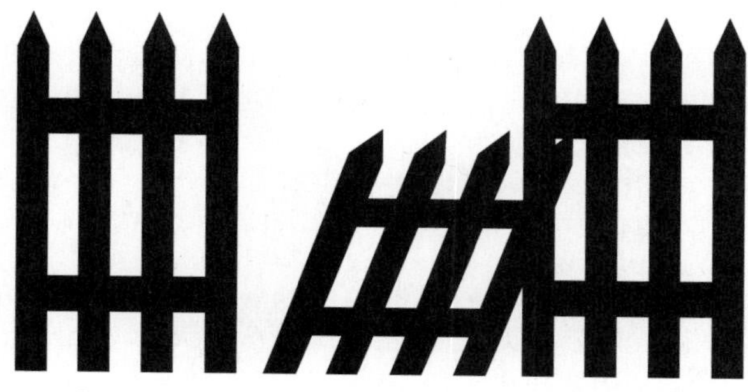

2. Give examples of a fence breaking down in one of these areas: sexual, friendship, personality differences, routine, life distractions. What is the condition of your fence? Does it need a fresh coat of paint or does it need serious repair? Examine the strength and weaknesses of your marriage.

Bibliography

Beach, Steven R. H., Evelyn E. Sandeen, and K. Daniel O'Leary
1990 *Depression in Marriage*. New York: Guilford Press.

Berman, Claire
1991 *Adult Children of Divorce Speak Out*. New York: Simon & Schuster.

Gottman, John
1994 *Why Marriages Succeed or Fail*. New York: Simon & Schuster.

Keirsey, David, and Marilyn Bates
1984 *Please Understand Me*. Del Mar: Prometheus Nemesis Book Co.

Lederach, John and Naomi
1991 *Recovery of Hope*. Intercourse: Good Books.

Penner, Clifford and Joyce
1981 *The Gift of Sex*. Waco: Word Books.

1997 *Men and Sex*. Nashville: Thomas Nelson.
Pipher, Mary
1996 *The Shelter of Each Other*. New York: Putnam Books.
Townsend, John, and Henry Cloud
1992 *Boundaries*. Grand Rapids: Zondervan Publishing.
Weiss, Lynn
1992 *Attention Deficit Disorder in Adults*. Dallas: Taylor Publishing Co.
Werner-Davis, Michele
1992 *Divorce Busting*. New York: Simon & Schuster.
Whitehead, Barbara DeFoe
1996 *The Divorce Culture*. New York: Alfred A. Knopf.

4

Freedom and Conflict in Marriage

If anyone can control his tongue, it proves that he has perfect control over himself in every other way. James 3:2 (TLB)

From the same mouth come blessing and cursing. James 3:10 (NRSV)

But the wisdom that comes from heaven is first of all pure and full of quiet gentleness. Then it is peace-loving and courageous. It allows discussion and is willing to yield to others; it is full of mercy and good deeds. It is wholehearted and straightforward and sincere. James 3:17 (TLB)

Conflict Is a Part of Being Human

James makes some interesting points about conflict. He recognizes the power of words to do both good and harm. He sees that there is a connection between words and actions. We have a choice as to how we will communicate our feelings and thoughts to one another. We use our freedom of speech to bless or curse. James sounds surprisingly in tune with our era by acknowledging the need for candor and flexibility in dialogue with others. It is remarkable that he had the courage to advocate openness while knowing the potential hurt that can come from uncontrolled words. James seems to be saying that openness is good but needs to be contained within boundaries.

Conflict is common in marriage. Conflict ranges from a direct yet respectful request for the spouse to place his or her dirty socks in the hamper to a volatile argument over who forgot to pay the mortgage. Some people deal openly and quickly with concerns. Others stew over stressful situations and then explode with emotions that they cannot repress.

Since spouses often come from families that are dissimilar, have personalities that usually are quite opposite, and have gender differences that are very challenging, it is hard to imagine a marriage without conflict. All of that plus having to deal with tensions over finances, children, personal habits, communication, and sex. It is a wonder that marriage works at all. Yet most people choose to marry and many stay married.

Eliminating all conflict is not possible. Nor is it even desirable because controlled conflict can even be helpful. We have conflict because we are human beings who are passionate and curious. We are people with opinions and needs. It is in the expression of our individuality that conflict takes place. The only way to avoid conflict is to have no opinions and no needs. There are probably not many people like that, and the few who try pay a high price by being diminished in spirit.

Sometimes an absence of conflict can look very inviting. However, it can mean that something is missing in the relationship. It is not whether we have conflict in marriage but whether we express it constructively or destructively that matters most.

Constructive Conflict

Most people enter into conflict with good intentions and for the right reasons. When they have a difference of opinion with their spouse, they honestly want to find solutions. They attempt to be flexible and to offer compromises. They are good listeners who work hard at resolving differences. They seek forgiveness and reconciliation. Conflict is a necessary step on the way toward being understood and respected.

Couples who handle conflict well are not frightened by it and are motivated to find a resolution. They do not like to live in tension. These couples know that conflict is never an end in itself and cannot be used to control or intimidate. Their experience tells them that constructive conflict can cause growth personally and in their marriage. People who handle conflict well are good problem solvers and put energy into finding solutions. They are aware of their own tendencies to mishandle conflict and take steps to correct what they do wrong. Becoming better at handling conflict is a lifelong process to which they are committed.

A Story About Constructive Conflict

Ken and Pat had a problem. In the fifteen years of marriage, they quarreled every year about where to go on their vacation. Ken was a rugged outdoorsman who wanted to go to a family hunting cabin in the mountains. He had gone there many times during his growing-up years and had fond memories of campfires, food, and night sounds. It was a cool place, both literally and figuratively. And besides it was free.

Pat was a beach person. Her family always rented the same place by the ocean when she was growing up. It was a tradition that had continued for several generations. The boardwalk, the smell of the salt water, and the warmth of the sun were a part of her memories. Her family shared stories throughout the year about the vacation. She was very close to her extended family, and the vacation at the ocean was a very important tradition to her.

In most respects, Ken and Pat were compatible, but they did have their differences. Pat was more outgoing and enjoyed people. Ken was more private and liked quietness. At the mountain cabin, Pat felt lonely and a little bit frightened. The bugs bothered her. The trees blocked out the sun. The long evenings were boring. She was expected to cook. She missed the excitement of the crowds at the beach.

Ken hated the shore. Too many people. The sun gave him a headache. The idea of lying on the beach was boring to him. He wondered why anyone would want to eat at a restaurant when they could eat home-cooked meals at the cabin. Ken missed his family gatherings and the touch-football games in the mountains. He felt out of place at the shore. Almost self-conscious.

For years Ken and Pat dreaded vacations because of the unresolved issue over where to go. For a while, they alternated each year between the families. But neither person felt satisfied. The disagreement spilled over into other aspects of their relationship. They started to feel some resentment for their in-laws. That led them to become defensive about their families and to attack each other with words. Their two children got drawn into the battle and felt pressed to take sides. The conflict began to take a toll on the marriage.

Because Ken and Pat had a deep commitment to each other, they chose to find a solution to the problem. They sought assistance from a counselor who helped them discover how they had been locked into positions that prevented problem solving. Because both felt comfortable with their childhood traditions and were loyal to their original families, they tried to extend what they had experienced as children into their own home. They discovered the importance of establishing new traditions that looked to the future more than to the past.

They were able to look for solutions instead of attacking each other. They then began to do creative vacationing. They rented a cabin by the shore in Maine.

They hiked part of the Appalachian Trail. They cooked for themselves and ate in restaurants. Even though their children still valued the extended family gatherings, they began to feel that this family unit mattered most.

It was because of the constructive conflict over family vacations that Ken and Pat chose to think more creatively about their own marriage. It helped them assume ownership of their relationship. It was more than just a continuation of the traditions of their extended families. Had they not conflicted, they would have settled for a pattern that could have been very limiting. If they had not resolved their conflict, they would have lived in increasing tension.

Conflict Is Constructive When It Helps Us Find New Ways of Doing Things.

It is too easy to stay with the familiar routines and not stray far from our comfort zones. When we play it safe, we do not grow. The wonderful contrasts in marriage are what make it new and fresh. These contrasts stretch us. The differences between spouses can give new energy and new ideas. Often one spouse initiates the stretching. That person tends to be more interested in change. The other may be more cautious. For that person, preserving the status quo is more important. However, both have a role to play.

It is in the arena of constructive conflict that growth can take place. Conflict is engaging. It is hard to ignore a spouse during a time of disagreement. For many people, it is an authentic moment of truth. When the conflict is handled correctly, new people emerge with better ideas. Ideas which may not have been discovered without the conflict. Constructive conflict can lead to epiphany. Avoiding conflict can lead to mediocrity.

Conflict Can Help Us Make Better Decisions.

Marriage is a complicated enterprise. In a lifetime, it

involves the earning and spending of large amounts of money. It is concerned with real estate and property management. It requires strategic planning. Often it demands that both spouses have sophisticated child-rearing skills. Spouses are dietitians and travel agents. They make critical decisions about the spiritual life of the family. And on and on. Is it any wonder that conflict happens in an organization this complex?

If conflict is inevitable, it is also desirable. One spouse alone often has trouble seeing the broad picture. Two perspectives are valuable. Decisions need to be debated. Ideas contrasted. In other aspects of public life, such as government, business, and the church, this often leads to sound decision making. Marriage is no different.

Conflict Can Make Us Better People.

No other setting has more potential for producing personal growth through conflict than marriage. It is within the safe, covenanted boundaries that individuals can take chances at disagreeing. More than in any other place, marriage can provide a setting for authentic conflict. Covenanted love creates an environment for taking risks at expression. For differing. For being confronted with disagreement. And for resolution. Partners feel respected when they are able to say what they believe, are heard, and are valued. They also grow when they create an environment of safe expression for the spouse.

Destructive Conflict

Embedded in the middle of conflict is the potential for good or ill. That potential is within every person and in every episode of conflict. Some people resolve conflict in a positive way. Those who do not harm both themselves and their marriage.

Abusive Conflict

The most pernicious forms of conflict are physical, emotional, and sexual abuse. They are morally and legally wrong. These forms of abuse are never justified, and abusers stand fully accountable for what they have done. Abuse is always hurtful to the recipient of the abuse and often places the marriage at a high risk of failure.

To Christians who believe in peacemaking and the dignity of other persons, all forms of abuse are an anathema. The church needs to continue to take a proactive role in preventing abuse and a supportive role to the recipients when it does happen. Abusers need legal constraints, professional treatment, and spiritual rebirth.

A Cycle of Destructive Conflict

A form of destructive conflict that needs to be better understood is the kind in which both spouses participate in a cycle of uncontrolled strife. The conflict is usually expressed both through inflammatory words and in attitudes of provocation. This kind of conflict cannot be resolved by focusing only on one spouse because both are active participants.

Each person must come to understand that the pattern is destructive and to recognize his or her part in the process. The relationship needs to develop new patterns of communicating in which spouses learn fresh ways to be friends and to be intimate. The energy driving the relationship must switch from one of contention to one of cooperation.

Common Destructive Conflict

Abuse and other forms of uncontrolled conflict are not common to most marriages. However, many couples do have their moments of destructiveness. These times are hurtful to spouses and to the marriage. Often it is expressed in harsh, penetrating words or in accusations and blaming. It can include long lectures that create a feeling of the "parent" scolding the "child."

Sometimes the most destructive conflict can happen when people use silence as punishment. We heard of a couple who had no meaningful conversation for three years because one had offended the other and refused to apologize. Often destructiveness takes place when either spouse becomes coercive and misuses power.

There are many ways of being hurtful. We all need to know our tendencies and take responsibility for correcting them. Destructiveness is a choice. While conflict is inevitable in marriage, destructiveness does not need to be.

A Story About Destructive Conflict

Ron is a very successful middle-aged owner of a small business. He is a high-energy person who is intensely competitive and enjoys high-risk activity. He grew up in a home where money was scarce and worry was abundant. His father struggled with a number of low-paying jobs and did not enjoy work or life. He was often irritable and was excessive in his punishment.

Ron's mother was frustrated by having to raise five children with very little money and not much help from her husband. She resented having to drop out of college because she was pregnant. In her frustration she would complain sharply to her husband.

Sue grew up poor. Her parents divorced when she was young. They fought bitterly before and after the divorce. She learned to survive through toughness and looking out for herself. She did not think she could trust anyone and kept everyone at a distance. What attracted her to Ron during her high school years was his self-confidence. He seemed to offer her a ticket out of a bad situation at home. While their courtship was quite sexual, it was not intimate.

Ron and Sue did fairly well with each other until the younger of their two children went to school. Ron was beginning to experience success with his business. That caused him to be away from home for long hours. At the same time, Sue lost her focus at home because the children needed her less during the day now that they were in school. Her life lacked meaning and purpose, and she went back to bed when the children got on the school bus.

Ron would come home from work to find dirty dishes in the sink and clothes unwashed. The house was a mess. The level of conflict picked up rapidly. Ron complained about her lack of productivity. She began to withdraw from him sexually. He started to drop hints about his secretary. She responded by neglecting her appearance.

Then the full-scale conflict began. First it was words. Harsh words. Accusations. Name-calling. Put-downs. Degrading words. Both spouses lost control. There were no boundaries. One day, Sue made a particularly harsh comment about the secretary after Ron criticized Sue for her weight. He responded by striking her across the face. Their fight was interrupted by a call from Ron's office. He left immediately and stayed away all night. The next day, a police officer served him with protection-from-abuse papers. One year later Ron and Sue were divorced.

Maybe Ron and Sue's marriage was a high-risk relationship from the beginning. The reasons for getting together were questionable. Marriage can never be an escape from a conflicted home life. It cannot be used as a refuge or as a healer of childhood wounds. Their dependence upon sex during the courtship allowed them to believe they were close when, in fact, they were not. They had little practice in problem solving and were not prepared for what was to come.

Ron and Sue fell into destructive patterns early in their marriage. They were not addressing the real issues and instead made the fight itself the focus. Their conflict could have been very useful if it had been directed correctly in the early stages. Solutions could have been found for Sue's emptiness. Ron could discover that life is more than material success. They could have learned to become intimate through resolving conflict. Instead, the way they handled conflict led them to believe that marriage cannot be a loving friendship. To them the only way out was through divorce.

Destructive Conflict: Causes and Solutions

Environmental Stresses

Destructive conflict takes place in some homes because the spouses are under too much stress. For example, their mortgage is too high, their work too demanding, and the children are out of control. These stresses create anger and anxiety that may not be expressed at the real source but may be deflected onto spouses or children. For example, if a husband is frustrated with his supervisor, he may not be able to tell him for fear of losing his job. However, that anger often comes out later at home. Often over small things that could have been handled easily without the carryover of work-based anger.

The same kinds of misplaced anger surface over worries about money. Spouses who are frustrated about bills cannot call the president of the bank to let off steam about the mortgage, but they can shout at each other for not putting the newspaper away. And when schedules are tight and there are too many things going on, few people confront the source directly. Instead of resigning from a committee, they become argumentative at home. Much of destructive conflict is a matter of scapegoating.

Some people call it "kicking the dog."

If conflict is to be managed we need to deal with the stresses in our lives. In the book, *Margin*, Dr. Richard A. Swenson talks about his decision to leave his private medical practice for a less demanding job to reduce his stress. It is his belief that we can protect the margins of our lives by making the hard choices about the uses of our time and energy.

Other people are giving up stressful jobs, cutting back on overtime, or reducing to one income. In addition, some couples are choosing smaller homes, holding onto the family car for an extra year, taking less expensive family vacations, or making other sacrifices for the sake of tranquillity. Some people need to resign from all committees during their most stressful years of marriage. Some couples decide that their children can only be in one sport or in one performance activity like piano. All outside intrusions into the home have to be examined carefully. Stresses can be managed but only if deliberate choices are made.

Wounds from Past or Present

Some conflict occurs when people carry hurts from the past into the marriage. When people feel wounded, abandoned, and abused, this pain often converts to anger and contentiousness. The source for the pain may come from the loss of a parent through death or divorce or from being away from home (i.e., boarding schools) for long periods of time at a young age. It may come from being punished too severely or from being abused physically, emotionally, or sexually. It may be a result of not being affirmed.

Some people continue to feel the pain of peer rejection while others experience failures that demoralize them. When these hurts are not resolved, they tend to surface in adult years as anger toward the spouse or themselves.

When our wounds contribute to conflict in marriage, they need to be identified and healed. Often that requires the objective help of someone who can see the bigger picture. That may be a friend or a professional who is a good listener and who can offer support. The listener can offer alternatives to the destructive methods that have been a part of the marriage.

The supportive church community can be very helpful in recovery and in representing the God of healing. John Trent and Gary Smalley's book, *The Blessing*, emphasizes the need people have to feel loved and special. When it is missing earlier in life, the blessing needs to be received from others in adulthood. People who feel cared for tend to be at peace. People who do not feel cared for tend to be in conflict.

Learned Methods of Destructive Conflict

Some destructive conflict is learned in childhood. Often from parents. The imprinting of behavior patterns takes place early in life and can remain through adulthood. Children assume that what they experience is the norm because they usually have few other models with which they can compare it. Thus, if parents engage in destructive patterns, children learn these methods of communicating and often carry them into their own relationships. We tend to behave in the ways we know best, even if those ways cause pain. As illogical as it may seem, these early lessons can brush aside objectivity, sensitivity, and even conscience.

If destructive conflict was modeled in childhood, new learning can take place. Parents who otherwise may have been loving, good people can still teach poor methods in handling conflict. Rejecting their methods does not mean rejecting them. New learning about what destructive conflict is and how to replace it with better methods is possible. It is important that new role models be found. Sometimes that can take place with friends, an older adult, a pastor, or a counselor. An in-law family can be helpful. Books, videos, and self-awareness groups can also provide ideas.

Destructive Conflict Is a Physical Process

Medical science continues to increase its understanding of the way the brain works. It is becoming clearer that behavior is directly influenced by the health and balance of the biochemistry of the brain. When we are fatigued or under stress, we tend to lose control more quickly. We become emotional, reactive, and argumentative. When stress becomes chronic and overwhelming, people can become emotionally unstable. Most destructiveness in relationships happens when the brain is out of balance. Sometimes the imbalance is short-term and easily corrected. At other times it is a part of an ongoing pattern of imbalance that may lead to frequent episodes of conflict.

Emotions are a part of a very complex environment in the brain involving hormones, electrical activity, genes, and other structural factors. Indeed, conflict itself can create an imbalance in the brain. Marriage therapist Dr. John Gottman explains in his book, *Why Marriages Succeed or Fail*, that conflict becomes destructive when people reach a certain level of physical reaction. For example, when the pulse rate becomes 10 percent higher than that person's normal rate, the conflict tends to deteriorate. Gottman believes it comes from the release of adrenaline that reduces the ability to think clearly.

To become better managers of conflict, we need to acknowledge the importance of maintaining healthy, balanced brains. When we are under stress, we will not engage in conflict. We will not argue at bedtime. In the midst of conflict, we will take breaks if our bodies begin to react physically. If we are prone to depression, anxiety, or perfectionism, we need to seek help because these conditions often lead to destructive conflict.

We may need to change the circumstances causing stress, find ways to restore balance to our brains, and in some instances seek medical help. We should never overlook the importance of a good night's sleep in preventing conflict. Sleep is the way the brain restores and rebalances itself. It can be helpful to know if there is a family history of conflict that may be based in genetic tendencies. Most of all we will want to consider our physical brains to be finite resources.

The Culture of Conflict

Conflict is a main theme in movies, plays, and on television. It draws increasing numbers of fans to spectator sports where violence is more important than the game. A hockey game without a fight causes some fans to feel cheated. Coaches who throw tantrums sometimes get more attention than the game.

The hosts of talk shows on radio and television build their audiences around a format of conflict. They invite guests who interrupt or physically attack each other. A generation of children is spending their free time playing video games or watching cartoons that are violent. As a society we are becoming a people who enjoy living vicariously through staged violence.

When violence becomes common, it can encourage abuse between spouses and toward children. As with many other things, small amounts may have little effect. But because it is so pervasive in the broader culture, it is hard to escape it. Perhaps we have come to accept anger as the norm. It is hard to keep it from becoming common in marriage.

As Christian peacemakers we must shape our environment in bold creative ways that reject the dominant culture. When we understand that violence is a product that is made for profit, we will choose other products. There are good movies and good television shows.

There are truly exciting sports. They deserve an audience. All of us enjoy being entertained some of the time, but it is very hard to justify participating in destructiveness as a spectator.

The Christian community can work harder to provide alternative forms of entertainment. It is important to reclaim the vitality of silence, of reflection, and of the inner journey. Jesus chose the wilderness and the garden for his retreat. Have we forgotten the wonderful mystery of the woods or streams? Therapist and author Mary Pipher, in *The Shelter of Each Other,* suggests to some of her clients that they watch the Nebraska sunset together instead of arguing. It is unlikely that we will think violent thoughts while feeling the waves of the ocean lapping at our feet. Destructive conflict is a choice. But it must be our choice to reject it. The world around us is inviting us to an environment of violent entertainment. We can choose a peaceful way.

Conflict is a part of marriage. Some of the time it serves a very useful purpose. Some of the time it is destructive. As Christians, James calls us be gentle, peace loving, and courageous in our interactions with others. To control our tongues and ourselves in every other way. We can determine the outcome of conflict by the choices we make. When we choose to be destructive, the results should not surprise us. In the same way when our conflict is constructive, we can enjoy the benefits of living in peaceful relationships. Most of all, we are at peace with ourselves and with God.

Freedom Fences

1. We will carefully manage our stress loads as well as our responses to unavoidable stresses.

2. If we grew up in families that handled conflict poorly, we will learn new patterns.

3. We will know our genetic history and become aware of the similar tendencies that affect us.

4. We acknowledge that our minds can be overtaxed and need adequate rest and healing.

5. In our attempt to manage conflict, we reject the culture of violence in which we live.

6. We will be deliberate in planning for constructive conflict. Couples will covenant together to uphold the plan.

Questions

1. When does conflict in your marriage lead to a good outcome or better solution? Share some examples.
2. What actions do you take that make conflict become constructive?
3. What conflicts are the easiest for you and your spouse to manage? The hardest? Why?
4. What stresses in your life that cause unnecessary conflict do you need to eliminate?
5. If your mind is not at peace and you know it is affecting your marriage, what keeps you from getting help?
6. How does watching violence affect you?
7. What should be in your conflict management plan?
8. How has your family of origin affected the way you respond to conflict?

Activity

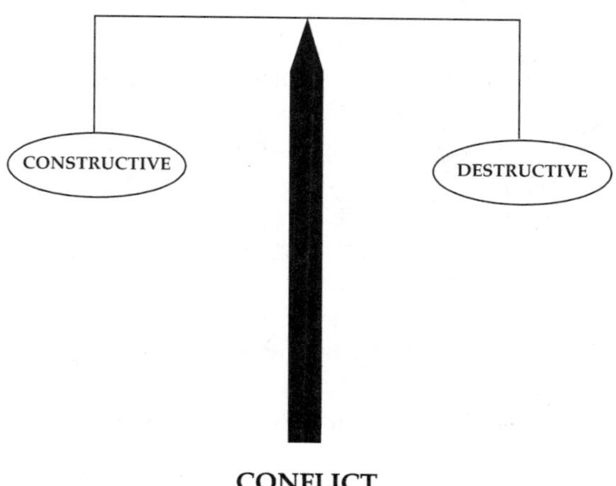

Name the influences in your life that contribute to destructive conflict. Identify those that produce constructive conflict. Put them on the conflict scale. What influences can you can add or take away to balance your scale? They may include:

Culture, stresses, pain, family patterns, physical issues, job, and others.

Rest, learning new patterns, anger, support, listening, medication, and others.

Bibliography

Fairfield, James

1977 *When You Don't Agree*. Scottdale: Herald Press.

Gottman, John

1994 *Why Marriages Succeed or Fail*. New York: Simon & Schuster.

Lerner, Harriet G.
1985 *The Dance of Anger*. New York: Harper & Row Publishers.

Miller, Melissa A.
1994 *Family Violence*. Scottdale: Herald Press.

Pipher, Mary
1996 *The Shelter of Each Other*, New York: Putnam Books.

Smalley, Gary, and John Trent
1980 *The Blessing*. Nashville: Thomas Nelson Publishing.

Swenson, Richard
1992 *Margin*. Colorado Springs: Nav Press.

Townsend, John, and Henry Cloud
1992 *Boundaries*. Grand Rapids: Zondervan Publishing.

5

New Roles in Marriage

There is neither . . . male nor female, for you are all one in Christ Jesus. Galatians 3:28 (NIV)

Now there are varieties of gifts, but the same Spirit; and there are varieties of services, but the same Lord; and there are varieties of activities, but it is the same God who activates all of them in everyone. 1 Corinthians 12: 4-6 (NRSV)

A Variety of Activities and Services

Your family is in the van on the way to church. Who is driving?

It is time for lunch. Who is in the kitchen putting the food together?

The house needs paint. Who is standing at the top of the ladder with a paintbrush in hand?

Your young child is upset and needs to be comforted. Who is there first?

A new sofa is needed. Who goes shopping?

The family is acting out a Bible story. Who is directing the activity?

What could Paul have meant about being neither male nor female? Are some roles done better by men or by women? Surely he was not suggesting that men should take over the kitchen or that women should climb ladders to paint the house. His advice to the

Corinthian church that they had a variety of gifts, services, and activities was encouraging. But he must have meant that they should be expressed within traditional gender practices. New freedoms in Paul's time or in ours are good in theory. Can they be taken too far in practice?

Traditional Roles

We all play roles in our marriages. Many roles. Roles are what we are supposed to do and who we are supposed to be. We are van drivers, cooks, and house painters. We are also comforters and decision makers. Did you ever stop to think about the things you and your spouse do? Do you ask yourselves why you do them or do you do them automatically without thinking?

Even though Paul raised the issue several centuries ago, many people are asking these questions now for the first time. Until the past several decades, roles were traditionally separated by gender, and people took very little time to process them. If people thought the "why" questions, they were rarely expressed.

Men did men's things. Women did women's things. It all seemed so clear. Surely there were exceptions on the farm where women sometimes had to help milk the cows, drive the tractor, and throw hay bales. Unfortunately, even if the wife stepped outside her traditional role, it was rare that the husband returned the favor by cooking the next meal or doing the next batch of laundry. Generally, roles were clearly maintained, even if there were some exceptions.

People undoubtedly read Paul's freeing words about gender, but they did not interpret them to mean that they should change their roles. Perhaps they were too busy doing the things necessary for survival to think seriously about roles. Besides, they, like all of us, were influenced by tradition.

Changing Roles

What a difference a generation makes! Today, roles are not assumed automatically, especially by many younger couples. Some would see gender-based roles as unfair, even as an injustice. Others might feel that some traditional restrictions keep them from fulfilling God's calling for them and from being free as Paul suggested.

Many believe role changes are necessary for their marriages to be complete. Increasing numbers of men are playing more active roles with their children. Some even stay at home to give childcare while their wives go away to work. Some women find a career outside the home to be more fulfilling. Clearly, roles are changing.

These days most couples need to talk about roles. For some the talk is brief and the decisions are prompt. For others the process is ongoing and the roles continue to evolve. Most couples know that change is in the air, and it is affecting them whether they want it to or not.

However, all of the changes are not without a downside. For example, some wives who succeed in getting their husbands to help with laundry duties still want the clothes folded their way. Some husbands who turn over the washing of the vehicles to their wives will want the Armor All applied "just so" to the tires. When sharing parenting responsibilities, one spouse can be critical of the way the other spouse handles the bedtime routine. All of this can lead to conflict over how the task is to be done. Change never comes easily.

Running a home is more complicated than most people think, and just when a couple believes they have the roles down pat, something changes. Sometimes that something is a new baby; a new job; or retirement. The problem with marriage is that it is always changing. When the changes come, it means going back to the drawing board. More talking. More processing.

There are some disadvantages when things are not automatic. While progress and change have a price, there certainly are advantages to becoming competent in tasks that are not traditional. People who can do a wide variety of tasks are freer than those who depend on others.

This happened for me when Marlene started her graduate work at age fifty-two. For those four years, I did most of the cooking, grocery shopping, and cleaning. I discovered that I actually enjoyed doing these things so much that I have continued to do them. Marlene was stretched too during those years. She was challenged and inspired by growing professionally. By becoming an income-producer. She took on new joy and stress as she faced the academic world and as she practiced a new profession. The changes caused us both to grow.

Gender Differences

Does our gender mean nothing when it comes to the roles we play in marriage? Surely there are characteristics that make one better suited than the other for certain functions. Certainly, God created the female body to be able to bear children and to provide milk for infants. God made most men to have a bigger physique to perform the heavy labor that was once required. Because of a height advantage, most men can see the dust on top of the refrigerator and most women cannot! Yes, there are differences. Some may be significant and some may not.

Most of the time, men and women are able to do the same things. There is not a male or a female way to load the dishwasher. There does not need to be a difference in the way a child is helped with homework. Maybe I do not look carefully as I drive through town, but I do not think I can tell whether the husband or the wife mowed the yard. If there are sections of the lawn missed, I assume a busy teenager mowed it. If roles are defined as things we DO, then basically men and women can DO the same things. It is really difficult to think of jobs that cannot be done by both. Some might argue that men and women do not do jobs equally well, but that may be a matter of opinion.

While our culture still connects women with cooking, some of the best chefs in restaurants are men. I recently had my car repaired by a relative who is a very good mechanic. The car runs quite well. That mechanic is a woman whose hands are just as greasy as her husband's. Some men are much better story readers for their children while some women are much more effective disciplinarians. Increasingly men are choosing to be elementary school teachers, and more women are becoming physicians. When the family checkbook needs to be balanced, sometimes it is the wife's job and sometimes the husband's. That role has nothing to do with gender. Are there many that do?

Perhaps some of the anxiety about the changes in roles comes out of a fundamental fear that these changes will cause the essence of maleness and femaleness to be lost. There is a concern that if men and women do the same things, dress alike, get their hair cut at the same salon, play the same sports, and do many similar things they will lose their uniqueness. Could it be that we are evolving into a genderless people?

However, all of these worries are about things people DO. They have nothing to do with who the genders ARE. This essence of maleness and femaleness is a mystery, and it is only a part of our BEING. Not our DOING. There are the obvious physical differences, but there are other differences as well. The problem is that the differences are much harder to pin down. Try describing this essence sometime without attaching it to the description of what that person DOES. It is hard to do. Society may change the rules about what genders can DO, but it can never change the essence of what genders ARE. Sometimes it is simply better to live with the mystery and enjoy the differences.

Personality Differences

An idea that is currently popular says men and women are different from each other in personality. That is to say, women act, think, and feel one way, and men a distinctly different way. As a figure of speech, they are said to come from "different planets." If they are different, is that difference biological? Some would suggest that hormonal factors can explain the variations between men and women. They point out that the predominate male sex hormone tends to make men more aggressive, while the predominate female sex hormone is more likely to make women more nurturing. Others point to a structural difference in the brain between men and women.

The idea breaks down because of its sweeping generalizations. If women are more emotional than men, why are all women not that way, and why are some men more emotional than some women? It is also said that men are more task-oriented, goal-directed, and competitive. That men always need to fix things. I think I know a few who are not like that. Probably you do too. Stereotypes so often get us into trouble.

Enlightened people lately have been trying to stay away from stereotypes when describing race, ethnicity, and social class. But for genders, are we restereotyping when we say "women are . . . " and "men are . . . "? The books about gender and personality may contain truths and may be entertaining. They may also put people back into boxes. Instead of being freeing, they can be limiting. Would they be in conflict with what Paul meant in his advice to the Galatians when he said, "In Christ, there is neither . . . male not female"?

The Many Tasks in Marriage

What are the various roles in our marriages? The list is quite long. So long that we do not get it all done. We lament that there is not enough time to do everything. Sometimes we feel guilty for not doing all of the roles successfully. But running a home is complicated. We tend to do the things that are the most demanding like cooking and cleaning. Or earning money. Sometimes it is house or vehicle maintenance that takes priority. Sometimes it is paying the monthly bills. Every family needs a transportation director and an activities director. Most families have an in-home health-care provider. Usually someone takes on the laundry service.

Because the list of roles and responsibilities is long and the time to do it short, couples tend to disagree about who should do it. There is a lot of pressure to get things done. If the school bus is in front of the house and the kids are still waiting for the dryer to deliver their socks, it can become a crisis. Some tasks may get overlooked because they are boring and tedious. We tend to blame the neglect, though, on our busy schedules. We may be partly right.

However, many roles are less clear-cut. For example, comforting a frightened child during a thunderstorm. That might not happen often, but it is still important. Then again, being a peacemaker between fighting children might be necessary every few minutes. That, too, someone has to do. Boosting the spirits of a spouse would be hard to write into a job description for marriage, but it may be one of the most helpful things one spouse can do for another.

Being an engaging partner in conversation is useful to marriage. So is having skill in planning interesting family vacations. Often if someone is the designated worrier in a family of risk takers or procrastinators, it is helpful. Somebody has to think of the "what if" questions. It is also helpful when someone plays a calming role to counterbalance the worrier. Even worrying has limited value. There are roles that can be listed on the refrigerator, and there are those which cannot. They are all important.

Functional Roles

The roles that can be posted on the refrigerator are for the daily tasks that are necessary to basic survival and comfort. These are the functional roles. They have to do with food, clothing, and shelter, and with providing the money necessary to maintain them. Every family needs to dedicate a certain amount of time to doing these tasks or the quality of its life can be adversely affected.

Obviously, there is a great deal of difference from one household to the next over how these tasks are done. Some families are very concerned with the physical aspect of their home life. Their houses are so perfectly maintained that everything is always in its place. Their budgets are so tightly managed that their families can go years between surprises. They are long on order but short on serendipity. For them, order is an end in itself, not a means to an end.

Other couples prefer unstructured living. For them

the functional tasks are an unwelcome intrusion. These families may "smell the roses," but may not weed them. Depending on serendipity causes them to miss the opportunities that can come from planned living. They may arrive at the airport just as their plane is leaving. Most people live between these extremes, but regardless where people are on the spectrum, roles relating to the functional needs are a part of every family.

Factors That Influence Functional Roles

1. It is crucial that couples decide what they value the most. If, for example, they are most motivated by material things, it may be necessary for both parents to work outside the home. Maybe even to work overtime. This may make it necessary to have some of the functional roles done by paid domestic workers. It may mean that more of the work will be done by the children. Most often it will be left for tired spouses. Although the extra income may allow the purchase of boats, expensive cars, or other things that are important to the parents, the trade-off can be poor meals, unkempt houses, and general disorder.

On the other hand, the outside jobs may provide the money that purchases family vacations or summer camp for the children. Sometimes it is used for education that enhances a career while at other times it is used for personal growth. Couples need to make decisions early in their marriage about what they value most. Their at-home roles will emerge out of those decisions. Often when families are in conflict, they have not matched their values with the roles. Sometimes people have chosen the wrong values.

2. Functional roles are usually done by the partner who has the most time. If the wife stays at home to care

for the children, she often assumes the responsibility for many of the household tasks. Increasingly, husbands who are wage earners assist with childcare when they are home. Or mow the yard, empty the dishwasher, change diapers, and many other tasks.

Some husbands need to be reminded that their wives also need recovery time, and that if they work together the tasks will be finished much more quickly and with everyone a lot happier. When both the husband and the wife work outside the home, the in-home tasks need to be shared fairly, even if one has a more demanding job.

3. Functional roles should be performed by the person who has the most skill and interest. Much of the time this point is irrelevant Sweeping is sweeping. It does not take much skill to clean out a bathtub. Skill levels do not even show up on the graph for most functional tasks. However, some things are extraordinarily important. Take good food for example. Increasingly families are catching a bite on the run. Maybe delivered pizza or prepared foods from a box. Often snack foods that are high in fats, salt, or sugar are low in nutrition. Good home-prepared food takes skill and interest. It is a skill that can be learned. It is a task that can be shared by parents. Certainly the primary cook deserves to be assisted by the spouse. The outcome is important to the family.

Some spouses are gifted at financial management. They need to serve as the treasurers. While the treasurers should discuss spending decisions with the spouses and keep them informed about the financial status, it is essential for the family to have one treasurer. When both are in charge or neither is, it is a formula for ongoing conflict. Other tasks like car maintenance, plumbing, and painting are vital parts of a well-functioning family. When cars are not dependable, faucets do not work, or the house looks run-down, families pay a price. They do not run smoothly, and both time and energy are spent compensating for weaknesses in these areas.

Obviously the spouse who has the skill in these areas will do the jobs. Fairness and balance should have little to do with the assignment of tasks in which one of the spouses has abilities that the other one does not have.

4. Functional roles are done best by plan. Most of the time the plan is unspoken but is understood by both spouses. Occasionally it needs to be talked over and clarified. Sometimes a family does best if they have a written plan posted on the refrigerator. Whatever the method, there needs to be a clear idea about which person will do what task. Good intentions alone may not be enough for most people. Many spouses need the Nike reminder to "just do it." An established plan may "swoosh" the undermotivated off the sofa and into action.

Sometimes when couples work on projects together, they can surprise themselves with how good this may make them feel toward each other. It may actually make them feel more intimate. For people concerned with communication skills or techniques for conflict resolution, they may get more satisfying results on opposite sides of a windowpane. Each with a bucket and sponge in hand. Undone tasks can corrode relationships as much as faulty listening skills. Couples need to work together as a team. All teams need strategies. They tend to win more when they do.

5. Couples can learn skills for new roles. A genera-

tion ago it was thought men did not belong in the delivery room with their wives because they would faint. When that myth was challenged, men learned to become competent coaches. Birthing babies has been made easier! Just as new parents have learned a better birthing process, they can also learn other skills like cooking, bathing children, mechanical awareness, and financial management. These skills will be learned only if both spouses are intentional about them and learn them.

Relational Roles

The most important roles in marriage cannot be posted on the refrigerator. These roles have little to do with the functional tasks of daily living. Nothing to do with the dishes, the car, or the yard. While there is a limit to the number of functional tasks in every home, the relational tasks are virtually unlimited. Functional tasks can be divided in a meeting around the kitchen table, but the relational roles cannot.

For many couples, the spouse's most important role is that of friend and companion. Long after the early fires of passion have cooled down, this role remains. Although this may be difficult for some couples to achieve, it is important that each spouse be the other's primary friend. The person you most want to be with. If spouses are not best friends, it limits their relationship. Other friendships are important but are always supplementary and never primary.

Spouses are in the best position to be sounding boards and reality testers for each other. Surely other persons can play this role, but no one can do it better than a spouse. There is a level of transparency that can only come from living together. The role of confidant should be unique to marriage. Marital partners can experience the highest level of trust and confidentiality. Except for situations of abuse or hurtful acts on the part of a spouse, privacy is a special privilege of marriage. No one else has a right to know the intimate story of a marriage.

The spouse should be the biggest encourager of the other spouse when it comes to learning, growing, and exploring. Stagnation from a lack of dynamic energy in the relationship will occur if the status quo is accepted. A spouse who cheers on the other spouse to new achievements plays a vital role. Spouses are exclusive lovers for each other. While this includes sexual love, it can mean an intimate love that can happen only in marriage.

The list of relational roles is endless. Fathering and mothering. Comforting, supporting, and disciplining. It involves spontaneous silliness as well as intentional wisdom and maturity. While these roles may involve DOING things for each other, relational roles have more to do with BEING things for each other. They are harder to learn because they extend outward from who we are as people. But they can be learned. That may be necessary when positive relationship roles do not happen on their own.

Roles in marriage can be constricting or they can freeing. Couples need to adapt to changes going on around them and to be responsive to the needs of their spouses and their children. The happiest marriages are the ones in which spouses are the most secure in their roles and are the most willing to be stretched past their level of comfort. Roles are never set in concrete.

Freedom Fences

1. We will celebrate our changing roles as we develop new gifts otherwise unknown.

2. We will learn new tasks in the household, even if it means less than perfect outcomes.

3. We will teach our spouses our unique skills without being condescending or mean-spirited.

4. We will avoid gender stereotypes and celebrate the differences between husbands and wives.

5. If overloaded, we will gently request assistance.

6. We will be attentive to the functional tasks our spouses do and be open to contributing more to them.

7. Knowing that relational roles are so crucial to a healthy marriage, they will be respected, nurtured, and cherished.

8. We will create a functional role plan by listing tasks or completing the quilt or other ways to be attentive to the importance of managing a household. See activity "Functional Role Quilt" at the end of this chapter.

Questions

1. What are the positive and negative aspects of traditional roles?
2. Which functional and relational roles cause you the most conflict? What compromises can you make?
3. With which relational roles do you have the most difficulty? Why?

4. What are some of the circumstances that make it difficult to be totally fair in our roles?
5. What do you think Paul had in mind in Galatians 3:28? Was he thinking about roles at all?
6. Imagine switching roles with your spouse for a month? How would the scenario unfold? Which of the functional and relational tasks would be most stretching? Impossible for you? How would the roles be better? Worse? No difference?

Activity

Functional Role Quilt

MOW LAWN			
	DISHES		CLEAN CAR
		GRAND-KIDS	
MAKE BEDS			
		WASH CLOTHES	
INCOME			

Step 1. List functional roles needed in your family household and put each role in a separate square. (Include the jobs held by wage earners.)

Step 2. Assign a different color for each participant: you, your spouse, each child, and each paid household service (cleaning, childcare, etc.).

Step 3. Estimate how much each person does in each role and color each quilt square accordingly. (Example: Cooking: wife 50%; husband 50%)

Step 4. Complete the entire quilt.

If this quilt is dominated by one color, what changes can be made to balance the tasks?

How would your life and the life of your spouse be affected by these changes?

Bibliography

Balswick, Jack
1992 *Men at the Crossroads*. Downers Grove: InterVarsity Press.

Elvenstar, Diane C.
1982 *Children: To Have or Have Not: A Guide to Making and Living with Your Decision*. San Francisco: Harvor Publishers.

Hochschild, Arlie
1997 *The Time Bind: When Work Becomes Home and Home Becomes Work*. New York: Metropolitan Books

Kraehmer, Steffen T.
1994 *Quantity Time*. Minneapolis: Deaconess Press.

Townsend, John, and Henry Cloud
1992 *Boundaries*. Grand Rapids: Zondervan Publishing.

6

Lifestyle Choices

I have set before you life and death, blessings and curses. Now choose life, so that you and your children may live. Deuteronomy 30:19 (NIV)

I am the true vine, and my Father is the vinegrower. He removes every branch in me that bears no fruit. Every branch that bears fruit he prunes to make it bear more fruit. John 15:1-2 (NRSV)

People Have Always Had to Make Choices

From the beginning of humankind, the way we live is presented as a choice. Free will is unique to humans. God reminded the children of Israel of the consequences of their choices. God did not hedge. It was life or death, blessings or curses. No in-between. No loopholes. The style of life we choose is of enormous consequence.

Thankfully, many of our daily choices are not that important. Imagine the stress load if we had to make life-and-death choices over what color our next car should be or whether we go to Vancouver, Maine, or to Cape Hatteras for vacation. These are not the kind of choices God was talking about. But many choices do matter. Some of them a lot. Perhaps that is why God acted so dramatically. God knew that if the language was fuzzy, we would not take choice making seriously. It is rather amazing that even with this kind of straight talk, the children of Israel did not always get it right. Neither do we. Among other things, poor choices can lead to divorce, bankruptcy, or life-ending disease.

One of the mysteries of the human condition is that we can stare in the face of death and still make choices that bring it on. It does not have to be that way. The informed human mind can be rational. It can choose life and blessing. Thankfully many do. This chapter is a plea to make life and blessing your choice.

Complicated Choices

Choice making is difficult because so many choices are complicated. What size house do we really need? Is it necessary to have two cars? Does it matter if our mutual fund has military hardware in it? Should we log onto the Internet and for what purpose? How do we choose between a job that pays well but requires extensive travel and one that does not pay adequately but allows us to be home?

These are the kinds of questions that confront us daily. They may not all be life-and-death choices, but they are still important. How we answer them will determine how our lives turn out. Our choices have outcomes. We cannot avoid their consequences.

While God may not directly punish us for our choices, neither will God always prevent the results. If we choose a house that is bigger than our income can support, the bank will take it from us. God will probably not put in a good word for us with the loan officer. The ultimate truth about lifestyle is that while we choose it, we rarely bear the consequences alone. Spouses, children, family, friends, the church, and the larger community share the benefits of good choices and the tragedies of the bad ones.

A Story of Family Lifestyle with Two Endings

Scott is very energetic. He is forty-two and the president of his own company, which he started from scratch when he was thirty. Marsha is forty and a teacher. They have been married for fifteen years. Their son, Chip, is fourteen and their daughter, Heather, is twelve.

The family lives in an upper-middle-class suburb on the edge of a major city. Their house has 4000 square feet of living space and an in-ground swimming pool. Scott drives a new luxury sports car and Marsha a two-year-old fully equipped van. They own a sailboat and belong to a yacht club. They are financially comfortable.

Scott and Marsha are members of the worship team at their church. Scott plays guitar, and Marsha is the lead singer. They enjoy the new style of music and believe that fresh life is coming to their congregation because the service is contemporary. They frequently share their spiritual story with the congregation.

Ending 1

When Scott's company passed 10 million dollars in annual sales, he wanted more. Scott announced to his managers that he plans to market their product nationally and double sales within two years. Reaching this goal would require sacrifice from each of them. They would be compensated through an increase in salary, but it could mean longer hours and, for some of them, additional travel. He stressed that loyalty to the company was expected. Their families would need to be supportive team members.

In the beginning of the business expansion, Marsha

was happy. She shared Scott's enthusiasm for expanding the company. She had come to appreciate the material benefits of success. In the winter she could play tennis three times a week with her friends. In the summer they would play golf and have lunch together. As a family, weekends on the boat were relaxing. The break from church was welcome because of the time and energy they felt church required of them.

Scott wanted the children to be rewarded for their sacrifices too. Chip was given his own JetSki to use at the marina. He took golf lessons. The parents enrolled Chip in prep school. He would be boarding there next year. Heather also benefited from the family success. She took violin and ballet lessons. The ballet instructor noticed unusual ability in Heather and suggested she take instruction with a well-known teacher in the city. She would be gone three evenings per week. If she did well, perhaps she could get summer instruction in New York.

The family began to disintegrate. Scott was rarely at home in the evening. He was entertaining clients much of the time. He began to golf often. He said it was for business contacts and to relax. Alcohol became important. Scott said his clients expected it. Church was becoming an intrusion. He was increasingly bothered by some of the criticism about his lifestyle. The worship team would have to go on without him. Scott stopped contributing money to the church because he did not like the way the church budget was being spent.

Marsha was losing friends. They saw her as pretentious and declined offers to play tennis and golf. She withdrew from the worship team. She felt alone. She missed Scott and began complaining. He made promises that he never kept. He reminded her that his hard work was providing nice things. Spiritually she was empty.

Chip and Heather felt abandoned. While they initially were excited with their lifestyle, it became hollow. The JetSki was no longer a thrill. During his first year at prep school, Chip was homesick. He did not think he fitted in with the other wealthy students. His grades went down. Heather could no longer maintain her friendships because she was always practicing ballet. Her friends moved on without her. Both Chip and Heather missed the youth program at church.

This family's lifestyle had changed. Where once they were bonded by their positive beliefs and values, they now allowed material success to separate them. Their new lifestyle brought a new set of values that were divisive and destructive. They were no longer family. They were no longer a part of the church family. They were on a journey away from God.

Ending 2

Because of their heavy commitments to work and church, Scott and Marsha made a decision to manage their free time carefully. They knew they needed time for themselves, with each other, and with the children. Knowing that money and possessions can control lifestyle, they tried hard to not let that happen. They occasionally felt guilty for being affluent and considered scaling down their lifestyle.

But they were comfortable with the good things their money allowed them to have and decided to give a 20 percent tithe as a way of sharing with others. They frequently hosted business acquaintances on the boat, and family and friends at home. They were gracious, giving people. They saw their wealth as an opportunity to share with others.

Scott and Marsha limited the children's outside activities. Chip only played basketball, and Heather only took violin lessons. The family spent a lot of time together on the boat, swimming, and playing golf and tennis. The children were encouraged to invite friends to be an active part of their family activities.

Scott and Marsha refocused their lives personally and spiritually. They managed their schedules well. They enjoyed recreation but kept it in balance. They rarely allowed boating to take them away from church activities. Most evenings, they were able to have a time for spiritual reflections as a family. All four of them participated in creating a worship moment. They planned events for contributing to people in need. They painted the house of an elderly man who went to their church. One summer they spent a week doing service work in Appalachia. They frequently talked about wealth and stewardship. The parents created an awareness of God's preeminence. They talked often about the pleasures of freedom and the rewards of restraint.

Lifestyle and Money

In one way or another, money affects everyone. It is hard to escape its power. While too little money can imprison people in despair, too much can imprison people in self-indulgence. Because money often determines lifestyle, it is important that we understand what we believe about it. Our beliefs shape our decisions about how much we think we need and how we use what we have.

Negative Uses of Money

Money is power for some people. They use it to control others. They try to buy their way through life with it. Money speaks, whether it is to get a special seat in a restaurant or a seat on the school board. Some affluent people expect that special privileges should be granted them. Money can bring them prestige. Occasionally their possessions are overly extravagant and ostentatious. Satisfaction may come to them more from the responses of people to their wealth than from the possessions themselves. Sometimes money is used as an escape from the routine and from the common. Wealth can buy boats, condominiums, cabins, and exotic vacations. All of these can give a sense of control over the environment. This control can buy freedom from congestion, waiting in lines, and the frustrations of the common person. Materialism, they argue, is good for the economy.

Positive Uses of Money

Money is necessary to meet the basic human needs: housing, clothing, food, and medical care. Money is needed to buy essentials. Poverty can demoralize the soul and jeopardize the body. Money also enables people to explore and expand their world. It allows for the purchase of books, travel, night school classes, and the good feelings that can come from discovery. It takes money to entertain and to socialize. Whether we invite people into our homes or to dinners in restaurants, we need money to make it happen. Many congregations raise large amounts of money to send their youth to church conventions. Part of the purpose is social.

Lavishness may not be necessary but specialness is. There may even be room for controlled extravagance. We so easily become uncomfortable with what may seem to be excess. Many of our ancestors had parlors in their homes that were used only on very special occasions.

In a sense, those rooms were excessive because they had no other use. They were not functional. The fancy china and dishes were brought out only for Christmas and Easter dinner. Special excesses can give special meaning. In a sense God is also excessive. How else can monarch butterflies and orchids be explained? Perhaps the ecosystems could have survived without them, but the human spirit would have been diminished. Beauty is to be created and enjoyed. Unselfconsciously.

Wealth, in whatever amount, is also to be shared. It has meaning only when a significant amount of it is given away. For many people this begins with the tithe. Others may choose different ways to share. Good things cannot be kept. They are celebrated when shared. The church and its institutions will prosper only when people share their wealth. People will prosper in spirit when they acknowledge that what they have is not really theirs anyway.

Money Management Issues

Money never manages itself. When we do not control it, it will control us. Many couples get into trouble because they have no money management plan. Their spending may be impulsive. Bills may get paid late or not at all. Credit ratings may suffer. The expensive costs of credit cards drive up their debt. Some people are addicted to spending.

A written budget is necessary for some people. They may need someone to help them manage their finances. Perhaps every congregation should have financial advisors who give guidance to members who have management weaknesses. While some congregations offer counsel to members in other aspects of their life, the same support could be offered in the financial area.

Couples in trouble financially are likely to be in trouble emotionally too. As a church community, we need to take the lifestyle patterns of each other more seriously. We can help each other when spending gets out of control and money is not handled well.

One of the most common conflicts in marriage is over the ownership of money. Traditionally men have been the primary wage earners, and some of them have seen the money as "theirs." They believe if they earned it they should decide how it is spent. Today more women are contributing financially. Because of that, some couples maintain separate accounts with complicated systems for paying expenses.

However couples choose to handle their money, it is important that they see their income as a common resource and make joint decisions about how to use it. Money becomes divisive when spouses are possessive about its ownership. From a legal standpoint, the money belongs to both. Spiritually God calls a couple to become one in every way.

Lifestyle and Recreation

Good forms of recreation are important to families. We need to get up from our couches, away from our television sets, and off of the Internet. We have become passive people who depend on being entertained. For some people structured recreation such as softball, volleyball, and competitive sports are meaningful outlets. Other people find satisfaction in the programs at health clubs, gyms, and the YMCA. These forms of recreation may be more satisfying because of the benefits of group participation and their competitiveness. However, they are usually done seasonally or just a few evenings each week. They are dependent on other people's schedules.

Activities that can be done alone or with a spouse, like running, walking, bicycling, or swimming, are much more practical because they can be done more frequently and with fewer complications. It is often possible to include children in these kinds of activities as well. Camping, hiking, and in-home recreation can be activities that draw family units together. Playful recreation and physical outlets are significant for personal and family health.

It is important that recreation be balanced with other family needs. Some spouses are involved in activities that take them away from each other too frequently. They are tied up many evenings and weekends. Their recreation patterns are not much different from when they were single. They may need to make compromises for the sake of the relationship.

When the need to remain active with old friends or to still feel the thrill of competition outweighs the needs of the relationship, it is important to examine the recreation choices. While some people need to be encouraged to be more involved in recreation, others need to learn new outlets with their spouses and families.

Lifestyle and Entertainment

People seek to be entertained. Life can become routine and monotonous without it. We want drama and intrigue. We are curious about the events going on around us. When there is not enough excitement in our lives, we create it through stories, plays, music, and games. Every society has its own forms of entertainment. It brings people together in community.

We laugh and cry together and learn from each other through entertainment. We can also be entertained in solitude by reading a book or watching a bird. Entertainment fills the empty spaces and enriches by stretching the mind and the soul. Entertainment is best when it strengthens marriages and improves the quality of family life.

North American entertainment has increasingly been influenced by professional sports as well as by the movie and television industries. Athletics has become big business with skill and teamwork becoming secondary to profit margins and financial contracts. The role of the athlete has been elevated to a level of hero worship. We have become a nation of professional spectators.

Movies and television continue to create a product that is aimed at the lowest common denominator. The plots are weak, and they depend on increasing levels of sexual exploitation and violence. The volume level gets louder, the language more profane, and the action more hyperkinetic.

Couples and families need to be critical consumers of both the sports and entertainment products. Some people spend entire Sunday afternoons watching professional football. Others sit in front of the television for entire evenings. Some see virtually every new movie that is produced. Not only does this style of entertainment generate passivity, but the values that are brought into the relationship are destructive. These forms deprive spouses and children of more meaningful time together. Family time is significantly compromised when there is dependence on these kinds of entertainment.

Lifestyle and Health

It is in the area of our health that many of us are confronted by the words of God to Moses to "choose life" (Deuteronomy 30:19). We often require the pruning that Jesus was talking about in the Gospel of John (John 15:1-2). We deal with health concerns every day. Many of the choices we make have direct impact on our lives. We take our health for granted when we engage in risky behavior. While in one sense we are only responsible to ourselves for our choices, we are asked to be stewards of the bodies given to us by God. And the impact of our choices always affects other people. In terms of health, individual choice is an oxymoron.

We are responsible for the substances we take into our bodies. Whether it is in our eating patterns, or the use of tobacco, alcohol, or illicit drugs, all will have some impact on our health. Most people have all the information they need to make informed choices about these substances and choose to ignore the fact that these substances are dangerous.

Some people engage in other high-risk activities such as excessive speed driving or dangerous recreational hobbies. Although they may find these activities challenging and exhilarating, does that justify them? Some people's health is jeopardized by their sexual choices. Promiscuity, even with safeguards, is always high risk. The only safe sex is with a lifetime partner who is disease free.

We are also called upon to choose life by managing our stresses, including getting enough sleep. As a people we have never carried more stress than we do today, and we have never been so sleep deprived. Falling sleep while driving is the second leading cause of death on the highway.

A lifestyle of health involves our choice making. In marriage the most loving thing we can do for our spouses and for our children is to choose carefully how we live. If as the passage in Deuteronomy 5:33 says, we want to live long on this earth, we will sacrifice some of our options to choose the freedom that comes from healthy living. We will be willing to submit ourselves to the Vinekeeper who prunes our lives to produce good fruit (John 15:1-2). A lifestyle of freedom within fences is one in which we acknowledge that we cannot "have it all" through material things, recreation, entertainment, or what brings the body pleasure. But instead we are fulfilled through contained living.

Freedom Fences

1. We will choose to have mentors who will offer honest opinions about our lifestyle choices.

2. As stewards of our money, we will manage it carefully and will not permit it to separate us from God or from others. We will share generously with those in need.

3. We will reject all forms of entertainment such as sexual exploitation, violence, and vulgarity that degrade and diminish the human community.

4. We will control the use of the computer Internet and its chat rooms, pornography, and addicting enticements. We will also place a time limit on the use of our computer. It will not take priority over our marital relationships or our relationships with our children.

5. We will choose forms of recreation that are safe, contribute to health, restore the mind, and strengthen marriage and family relationships.

6. We will make lifestyle choices for health that respect the body and its delicate balances. We will accept that all lifestyle health choices are essentially communal.

Questions

1. In what ways do your lifestyle choices affect those around you?
2. How do you decide which lifestyle issues really matter and which are just a personal opinion?
3. What role does the church have in helping people with lifestyle decisions?
4. Why does money harm some people and not others?
5. Why is it necessary for couples to spend their playtime together?
6. When one spouse refuses to change personal health habits, what should the other spouse do?
7. What is wrong with watching a lot of television?
8. What lifestyle issues concern you? What changes can you make to make your life more complete?

Activity

Tree

Place lifestyle choices on your tree and evaluate how they bear fruit in your life and in your family. What needs to be pruned in order for changes to occur? Lifestyle choices include the following: work, money, possessions, recreation, entertainment, food, exercise, toxic substances, Internet. Add others that are important to you.

Bibliography

Hunt, Mary, ed.
1998 *Cheapskate Monthly*. Paramount: Hunt Publishing Co.

Kelley, Linda
1996 *Two Incomes and Still Broke*. New York: Times Books.

Kraybill, Donald
1990 *The Upside Down Kingdom*. Scottdale: Herald Press.

McGinnis, Kathleen and James
1990 *Parenting for Peace and Justice*. Maryknoll: Orbis Books.

Miller, Lynn A.
1991 *Firstfruits Living*. Scottdale: Herald Press.

Pipher, Mary
1996 *The Shelter of Each Other*. New York: Putnam Books.

Schor, Juliet B.
1998 *The Overspent American*. New York: Basic Books.

Swenson, Richard A.
1992 *Margin*. Colorado Springs: Nav Press.

Sine, Tom
1994 *Live It Up!* Scottdale: Herald Press.

Wylie, Mary Sykes
1997 "Our Trip to Bountiful" in *The Family Therapy Networker*. May-June.

7

Balancing Work and Family

There is a time for everything, and a season for every activity under heaven. Ecclesiastes 3:1 (NIV)

Do not work for food that perishes, but for the food that endures for eternal life, which the Son of Man will give you. John 6:27 (NRSV)

Working for Survival

The only satisfaction Jerry's father, Cal Kaufman, found in his toilsome labor in the coal mines of western Pennsylvania was the meager envelope of cash he picked up from the paymaster at the end of the week. In the 1920s and 1930s, there was not much else he could do to support his family. Times were hard. For Cal, work meant spending ten-hour days deep within the bowels of the earth, lying on his belly with a pickax in hand. Every day he was confronted with the possibility of a collapse of the mine roof, being trapped and entombed, or of an explosion of methane gas. The coal dust he breathed eventually contributed to his death.

There was no such thing as career counseling to help

him find more fulfilling work. Cal and his co-workers did not give much thought to their inner needs. The word *burnout* had not yet been coined. Workers were mainly concerned with their survival and the economic survival of their family. They had few choices about work.

Until recent times, people worked only to provide food, clothing, and shelter. The thought of working for pleasurable items or diversions was never considered. When the industrial revolution arrived, it created many new occupations, although work was still seen as a way to provide for the basic material needs of the family. Working to support leisure-time pleasures or for personal satisfaction is a recent invention. Advances in technology and affluence have profoundly changed the meaning and purpose of work.

Many people still work mainly for income. They have no particular career goals in mind. A job is something a person DOES, not something a person IS. Work has little to do with enhancing self-image. For many, their jobs are simply tools that enable them to pay for food, housing, and clothing. Not much else. They live from paycheck to paycheck with little hope of escaping the cycle. Work has little meaning beyond this.

Working for More Than Survival

For others, the meaning of work has changed dramatically since the 1960s. As the Western world entered the postindustrial era, jobs have changed as well as the attitudes of the workers. Society has become high tech, and education has become increasingly important in our jobs. Prosperity and lifestyle expectations have increased immensely. Work has become a way of buying the good life. Having bigger houses, swimming pools, eating in restaurants, traveling extensively, owning vacation condos, and having two cars in the garage are some of the things people expect to buy with their money. Even for families on the lower end of the pay scale, there are some perks for their hard labor. They too, eat out frequently, if only in a restaurant with a more modest menu. They may camp on their vacations or stay in less pricey places. Entertainment forms have been created to suit the wallets of all income levels. The good life comes in many different ways.

Now that most North Americans do not have to work just to survive, there has been an escalation of desires. Perhaps it is a part of the human nature to always want more. A generation ago, the average couple had twice the number of children and a house with half the size of today's families. Presently many houses are filled with the inventions of modern technology. When my father came home from the mine, he relaxed by listening to the radio in the living room. Today our home has three television sets, a stereo system with compact disc player, a video camera and VCR, and a computer hooked into the Internet.

Traveling to Europe or skiing in Colorado would have been the last thing my father would have considered. He never heard of saunas. A weight room at his workplace would have gone unused because the men had pumped all the iron they needed with shovels and pickaxes. As our incomes have exceeded the basic survival needs, a world of commerce has emerged that invites all of us to feed at a new table. Not at the table out of need but of desire. For many it has become a banquet.

As this table has grown larger, so have the expectations that our work will provide the income necessary to maintain the new standard of living. That means more education, training, and retraining. It also means longer hours. And for many, it requires two incomes. Because it is hard for many people to down-scale their lifestyle once they have reached a certain level, they choose to work more to pay for what now seem like necessities. While Jerry's father worried that his pay envelope would not have enough in it to pay for food, today's workers have new things to worry about. They want computer upgrades for their junior high children, the best summer basketball camps, cars for their teenagers, or keeping up with credit card debt. For them success is measured by having more of everything.

Career Expectations

Workers have expectations that their jobs should put them on career paths that are going somewhere. They believe that if their careers are stagnant, they are going down dead-end streets. Growth and advancement are the expectation. While these have little to do with putting bread on the table, they have everything to do with the expectations to market their skills elsewhere. To avoid career flat-lining, workers put in more time, show more intensity, play more golf with the boss, take more work home, and make more compromises of the soul. These activities build good résumés. But at what price?

Have we forgotten the real meaning of work? That it is just for a season? Work can only ever be a part of the reason we are here. Maybe even a small part. The food that it provides needs to be eternal for our work to fulfill God's calling. God does not place us in this world to climb the corporate ladder or to achieve material success. The reason that God gives us for work is related ultimately to the purpose for which we are called.

Modern Benefits of the Workplace

The pay envelope today has more than coins in it. That envelope includes rewards for the psyche. The feeling that the worker is special. Important. Even indispensable. Work is no longer to provide just for the essentials of survival. Workers today believe that their careers should enable them to achieve their highest potential. Motivation experts are hired to tell them so. They expect that their work should be a "feel-good" experience. Feeling negative does not fit the company mission statement or help reach the long-term goals. The belief is that people who feel good about themselves do better work. Some would see the workplace as therapy or as the great place to become equal or superior to others. Country and western singer Tennessee Ernie Ford sang during the 1950s, "I owe my soul to the company store." He was referring to his economic and emotional dependence on the coal mines where he worked and at whose stores he bought his families' necessities on credit. Today some workers are in debt to the company store. A different store but a similar debt. Work has different ways of owning the soul.

Honorable work can have real meaning. It does not need company cheerleaders to make that point. Satisfaction from work comes from doing things that contribute to the good of the community. These include making products like magnetic resonance imaging machines that enable physicians to see inside the body more accurately. Also important is doing public service like repairing power lines that have been knocked down during a storm. Meaningful work does not need the hype of motivators. It produces its own satisfaction.

Most work has dignity because it serves a noble purpose. Most of us could not live well without people who pick up our trash or without highway workers who plow the snow from our highways. Ever since Adam and Eve left the garden, there has been work to do. God gives us work because it needs to be done and work gives us meaning. People get restless when they are laid off from a job. They feel despair when they cannot find work. Sometimes workers' interests and their jobs do not match. They may need to retrain for another area. However, when people are doing honorable work and it is compatible with their interests, they feel fulfilled.

Choices

The jobs themselves are more rewarding because society is much more diversified. The spectrum of opportunity is broader because of the explosion of technology and knowledge. Not to mention the vast expansion of the marketplace of goods and services. Several generations ago, the number of jobs and professions done by people could have been written on a few sheets of paper. Workers had few choices. The people who were farmers or nurses might have wanted to do something different, but it mattered little because their opportunities were limited.

As society has become more complicated, the list is much longer. The problem is how to choose from a vast number of careers. People can train for jobs that are creative, use their minds, serve people, and even fulfill a spiritual calling. With the fluid, changing work environment, many workers are retrained for second and even third careers. It may be unrealistic to believe that people will have one job for a lifetime. This reality impacts the marriage and family life in part because career now has become a primary focus for the worker. In a very real sense family now competes more than ever for the loyalty and energy of the worker. For Jerry's father the work in the mines did not compromise his commitment to the family. However, many of the jobs in today's market are interesting, challenging, and require the worker to make critical choices about loyalties.

Women and Minorities

Women and minorities today have a greater access to careers. With the proper training and personal skills, any adult can do almost any job. Opportunity is now theoretically equal for all people. White male privilege is diminishing. Old biases about who is suited for particular jobs are fading. Some would say these changes have not been fast enough or complete enough. However, change is occurring. African-Americans are owning more businesses. Equal numbers of women and men are entering medical school. The potential of workers is not as restricted by arbitrary boundaries as it once was. The impact of this change on marriage and family life is significant.

Increased Prosperity

The increases in income have provided valuable additions to contemporary lifestyle. While materialism has a downside, much about the current prosperity is positive. Conveniences make life easier. Not many people would want to wash their clothes on a washboard again or ride a horse to work. The telecommunication system is vastly superior to the Pony Express. Many people choose travel that is educational and brings them into contact with people from other cultures. Our extra money can buy us good things. When they are bought for the right reasons and are not excessive, we need not feel apologetic. But prosperity has a downside.

The Price for the Worker

Even satisfying work produces stress and fatigue

that robs workers of the opportunity to spend meaningful time in regeneration and creative activity. Workers may live off of adrenaline, but only for a time. Unfortunately, people who like their work are often unaware of how unbalanced their lives have become. Some of them keep drawing from a well that is already dry. The insidious thing about even good work is that it can be bad for people.

For generations, men have had to make personal sacrifices as principle wage earners. Some paid the ultimate price with their lives and some with serious illnesses, such as lung diseases from exposure to asbestos. The weight of providing for the family financial survival was heavy for many men because they were the sole wage earner. There was no other choice. Even today, most men continue to be the primary providers. With the upscale living expectations, that burden remains.

Historically, women too have carried a heavy workload in raising children and managing a household. They did not receive pay for their twenty-four-hours-a-day job. Whether or not to have a large family was often not a choice. Birth control is a relatively recent development. As increasing numbers of women enter the paid workplace, they too feel the same stresses men do. In addition, they often have the primary responsibility for managing the household and caring for the children. Some women work outside the home because their income is needed for essentials or it pays for extras. Some women choose to work primarily for emotional and career reasons. When the family lifestyle gets built around two incomes, options for women to reduce the stress in their lives also diminish. They can feel just as trapped as men do.

The Price for Marriage

Work impacts marriage. It can take time and energy out of a relationship. It can interfere with communication and leave less energy for romance. Tired spouses are often less creative and spontaneous. Work is increasingly influencing the shape of intimacy. Whether it demands longer hours or increased loyalty, work has become a silent third partner in many marriages. When couples gave their solemn pledge at their wedding to "let no-one put the marriage asunder," they were thinking only of people who might enter the relationship. Few of them would have thought of their work as an intruder. But for many people, work can be as damaging. This has happened in part because employers have created a work environment that is so comfortable for employees that home-life looks less appealing. The company gym beats mowing the yard by a landslide! Arlie Russell Hochschild's book, *The Time Bind,* describes how work has become home and home has become work.

The workplace has indeed become a threat to marriage through the widespread mixing of men and women. Workplace-generated affairs are becoming more common because workers spend more of their waking hours with each other than they do with their spouses. Often people look their best and are in their best persona while at work. Spouses can be at a disadvantage with these relationships because they are a part of the real world at home.

Workplace friendships of the same gender can interfere with marriage when the relationships extend beyond the work hours. As positive as these relationships may be, they need to be contained. The demands of the job itself are already taking time and energy away from the marriage. Workplace friendships can diminish the privacy of the marital friendship.

Job-related travel and shift work can weaken marriage by taking spouses away from each other during prime time. Many couples are like ships passing each other in the night. It is very hard to sustain the marital bond in absentia. Frequently couples who are separated in these ways experience a kind of grief over the loss of emotional intimacy. As with grief from the death of a loved one, feelings of connectedness eventually decline. Marital love can die from spouses being apart too much.

The Price for Children

The working hours of parents impact children. In the past, fathers gave marginal time to parenting in part because of their responsibilities as wage earners. They believed their primary role was to provide income for the family. Unfortunately, many fathers still see their role with that same single focus. A major change in recent years is that mothers are now also working outside the home. Many of them have difficult jobs and come home tired. In the past, jobs diminished the parenting contributions of fathers. The present trend is leading mothers down that same road. Jobs are becoming primary in family. Parenting is becoming secondary.

The irony is that just a few short years ago, child health experts were recommending the closing of orphanages and other institutions for children. Children in foster care were returned to their birth parents or placed for adoption as quickly as possible because it was assumed that children needed to be cared for by their parents. Institutions were out. Family was in. Today large numbers of mothers are leaving the home to work. Not many fathers are electing to stay home in their place. Daycare centers and other forms of substitute care have returned as institutional caregivers for children. Even though this substitute care is part time, it removes children from parents during the prime part of a child's day and at the most critical time of development and bonding.

When both parents work away from home, both bring home the fatigue and the problems of the workplace. Weekends are often filled with catch-up responsibilities around the house instead of building a playhouse for the children in the backyard. The pace for the whole family can be intense. When parents choose to have careers outside and inside the home, they need to be committed to work together as a team. They also need to make sacrifices in their personal free time, hobbies, and outside friendships in order to maximize their time with their children.

A television commercial shows a harried professional mother struggling with children who are wanting to go to the beach on a workday. She explains to them that she cannot because she has to see a client. When the daughter asks the mother if she can become her client, the mother is overcome with guilt and takes them to the beach instead of going to the office. As warm and fuzzy as the beach scene is, it is compromised by the mother who takes her cell phone along and talks with the client there. This vignette describes so well the marginalization of parenting. A client is still a client whether in the office or on the beach. Fathers have been stretching those limits for a long time. Mothers are now struggling with the same dilemmas.

Often when both spouses work outside the home, they do so believing they need to do so to pay their bills. "The two-income myth has convinced almost two-thirds of America's married couples that when money matters, a second paycheck is the best solution. Yet the trade of time for money hasn't always been a bargain"

(Kelley, *Two Incomes and Still Broke,* Times Books, p. 209). Linda Kelley suggests that unless the second income is quite high, the family will be left with little extra money after the transportation, childcare, taxes, and other expenses are calculated. In some cases, the second job may actually cost more than it earns. Couples must honestly discuss their motives for working outside the home. What are the rewards? What are the costs? What are the short-term and long-term effects on them, their children, and society? How much money does the family truly need to earn while the children are young?

Full-time Parenting as a Career

Most women receive the same level of education and training as men in their late teens and young adult years. Access to jobs is almost as good for women as for men, sometimes better. Women are valued as competent and skilled workers. By their late twenties or early thirties, many women are experiencing professional success. The thought of either the man or woman stopping their careers in order to care for children seems out of date. Stay-at-home parents may worry whether they will be able to restart their careers after the children go to school. They may wonder what they would do all day at home with a baby. It can be a difficult transition to go from a position where they received financial and personal rewards for their expertise to an unpaid and underappreciated role as parent.

There are daily rewards from seeing our children take their first steps or hearing them sing "The ABC Song" for the first time by themselves. But most of the time, the parents do not experience great satisfaction from cleaning up the half-eaten peanut butter and jelly sandwiches. Rarely are they commended for peacefully settling disputes between two siblings over who gets the purple cup and who gets the green one. Often parents at home feel isolated and undervalued. They dream about the days when they went to work, completed jobs, and received remuneration for their work.

So why do we advocate for full-time parenting? Yes, daycare standards have never been higher. Children can learn from the organization, purposefulness, and stimulation of these providers. Yes, grandparents and other relatives can be dedicated, caring, and available. Other people can take good care of our children. Our children may adjust to the setting. There are contradictory studies showing the positive or negative effects of utilizing outside caregivers. Some say children are better learners if they have been in daycare. Some say children have more childhood illnesses if in daycare. Others point to an increase in childhood depression, hyperactivity, and violence. They wonder whether it is connected to the decreasing contact between parents and children.

We are not here to promote the latest studies. We want to encourage today's parents to be the best they can be to their own children. For their own sake and most importantly for their children's sake. Parents have worked hard on their careers and on other relationships. Now it is a season for working hard on our relationships with our children. We know our children better than anyone else, and most of the time we will be the best caregivers for our children. If we want them to have the best toys or best education, why do we not want them to have the best parenting? Becoming a parent is an invaluable experience of putting another's needs ahead of our own. It is about weeding out what we thought was important and learning about simple pleasures. It is about learning the awesome developmental process of a baby growing into an adult. Parenting does not have to be a dull time. If we dedicate ourselves to learning how to be effective parents and build a network of support around ourselves, these years of being focused on raising our children can be the best years of our lives and the most secure and thriving period for our children.

Creative Solutions

Some adults are finding that parenting is only a brief part of their entire adult years. They are discovering it can be better to have a number of careers throughout a lifetime rather than one continuous career. Parenting is an important career. There is time for other careers. Although traditionally full-time parenting has been done by mothers, some couples choose to have the father be the primary parent. Some couples job-share so they can each be with the children part of the time. Some men and women have part-time businesses in their home.

If one parent chooses to be at home with the children, that parent needs to find ways to develop other skills and interests. These may be used for their own personal fulfillment or may enhance a career in the future. Volunteering at church or in the community is a wonderful way to have meaningful connections with the adult world. Stay-at-home parents have to manage their time carefully. Even full-time parents can put personal needs ahead of the children's needs. In order to thrive, every parent needs outside involvement. As charming as children can be, they can also drain parents. Carefully chosen outlets for creativity, exercise, and work can enhance parenting energies.

Time

No outside job, no matter how important, has a right to demand excessive time. Juliet Schor's book, *The Overworked American,* describes how the average worker is putting in 10 per cent more time at work than people did twenty-five years ago. Feeling guilty, we have created myths like "quality time" to soothe our conscience when in reality quantity is necessary for quality to take place. Children feel marginalized by parents who choose to put work ahead of them. Steffen T. Kraehmer's book, *Quality Time,* emphasizes the importance of time in creating bonds with children.

Marriages run dry from lack of time. As Christians, we are expected to be good stewards of marriage and family. It is a fragile resource that only we can nurture. Nobody can do it for us. When we allow work to intrude into our family time, we make a choice to place the family below our jobs in importance. Our work should account for about one third of our time during the workweek. The rest of the time is left for sleep, family, and other activities. Surely there are exceptions like farmers during seasonal work or professions like accounting during tax season. But when work routinely gets stretched beyond healthy boundaries, marriages and family life suffer.

Freedom Fences

1. We will seek jobs that benefit the community, are marriage- and family-friendly, and fulfill both financial and spiritual needs.

2. While we will find meaning in our work, it will only represent segments of our lives. We are defined more by who we ARE than by what we DO.

3. Bi-vocational parents will be unusually devoted to parenting when not working at their other

jobs. That means that during the prime parenting years, bi-vocational parents will minimize their involvement in hobbies, church work, and other friendships.

4. Parents who choose full-time parenting should be validated for this chosen career. They can use their time to participate in meaningful friendships and activities outside the home. They can return to their other careers at a later point. Volunteer opportunities can provide an outlet for professional skill and personal gain.

5. We will not allow the demands of the outside careers to consistently take time, energy, and loyalty away from marriages and families.

6. The perks of the work place will not be permitted to detract from the needs and rewards of families.

7. We will contain work friendships. Cross-gender friendships will be viewed with caution.

Questions

1. Why should work provide more than a means of survival?
2. What kinds of things make work meaningful?
3. How can we know when work is interfering with family?
4. How do family responsibilities affect career choices?
5. How can you tell which parent is best suited for providing primary care for the children?

6. Who can help us decide where to put the fences around work?
7. What benefits do you receive from your career?
8. What costs, financially and emotionally, do you experience from your career?
9. How can you decide what is "essential" versus what is personal "desire"? How does that support or contrast your choices around work?

Identify and prioritize goals in the following areas

	FINANCE	CAREER	FAMILY	CHURCH	COMMUNITY
TODAY					
5 YEARS FROM NOW					
10 YEARS FROM NOW					
20 YEARS FROM NOW					

Activity

Make a list of your current goals for finances, career, family, marriage, church, and community. Prioritize which are most important to you. In other columns, rank them for 5, 10, 20 years. Do they look different or are they the same?

Bibliography

Bielski, Vince
1996 "Our Magnificent Obsession" in *The Family Therapy Networker*. March-April, p. 22.

Bolles, Richard Nelson
1997 *What Color Is Your Parachute*? Berkley: Ten Speed Press.

Brownlee, Shannon, and Matthew Miller
1997 "Lies Parents Tell Themselves About Why They Work" in *U.S. News & World Report*. May 12, p. 58.

Hochschild, Arlie Russell
1997 *Time Bind: When Work Becomes Home and Home Becomes Work*. New York: Metropolitan Books.

Hummel, Charles E.
1994 *Tyranny of the Urgent*. Madison: InterVarsity Press.

Kelley, Linda
1996 *Two Incomes and Still Broke*. New York: Times Books.

Kraehmer, Steffen T.
1994 *Quantity Time*. Minneapolis: Deaconess Press.

Shapiro, Laura, Anne Underwood, Patricia King, Pat Wingert, and Claudia Kalb
1997 "The Myth of Quality Time" in *Newsweek*. May 12, p. 76.

Schor, Juliet B.
1997 *The Overworked American*. New York: Basic Books.

Spears, Larry C., ed.
1996 *Insights on Leadership*. New York: John Wiley & Sons.

Swenson, Richard A.
1992 *Margin*. Colorado Springs: Nav Press.

8

Spiritual Fences for Freedom

He tends his flock like a shepherd: He gathers the lambs in his arms and carries them close to his heart; he gently leads those that have young. Isaiah 40:11 (NIV)

"If you hold to my teachings, you are really my disciples. Then you will know the truth, and the truth will make you free." John 8:31-32 (NIV)

The Purpose of a Sheep Pen

Our daughter, Anne, herded sheep on the Navajo reservation in Arizona one summer while fulfilling cross-cultural credits for college. She, along with several other students, received a crash course in sheep herding. Then they were turned loose with sixty sheep and goats. After an arduous ten-mile loop through rocky crags and peaceful valleys, the students brought the sheep home safely. Even though the family had a sheep pen, they told the students to let the sheep graze around their house while everyone went inside for supper. When they came out an hour later, the sheep were gone. There was full-scale panic! Where had the sheep gone? Were they safe? After everyone fervently searched for several miles, the sheep were found, escorted home, and placed securely in the corral. The students and the Navajo family were extremely grateful and relieved that the sheep were safe.

Erecting Spiritual Sheep Pens

We too depend on the Good Shepherd to lead us, other sheep to walk with us, and sheep pens to contain us. Some of us like this system. We like to be in the corral and enjoy the food, water, and comfort of being at home. We make time to listen to the Shepherd and respond to his leadership. Others of us are constantly looking beyond the fence and seeing the vast expanse of opportunities we are missing. Some of us are better able to handle life outside the safety of a fence than others. Some repeatedly get caught in the briar bushes. As a society, we continuously struggle with wanting boundaries. On the one hand we want them and on the other hand we try to break free from them.

During the decades of the 1960s and 1970s, waves of antiauthoritarianism swept the country and took many of our spiritual and lifestyle fences away. Most Christians readjusted their beliefs to include more open stances on various issues. While the old systems may have been too rigid and too focused on arbitrary external constraints, a void was left when they were not replaced with a proactive theology of boundaries. Many people were so relieved by not having to follow the code that they became victims of freedom. They may not have experienced God in the confines of a narrow religious sheep pen but neither have they found peace in the endless meadow of unrestricted grazing land.

As Christians, we will at times make the fence too constrictive, but not having fences at all places us in peril. We have to involve head and heart in freedom fence building and continue to open ourselves to God's guidance in the process.

The Search for God

It is only by focusing on the Good Shepherd that we can begin to navigate a faith journey. We tend to focus on the borders of the sheep pen instead of looking for the guidance and comfort of the Shepherd within the pen. There are times to linger inside to be renewed, and there are times to explore the perimeters. The key is to remain close to the Shepherd. The closer we are to the Shepherd the less need we will have for rules and boundaries.

We will not want to stray. We will not take unnecessary risks. We will not follow the voice of an intruder because we will know our Shepherd's voice. Galatians 5:13-15 tells us that we are called to freedom but that we should not use our freedom as an opportunity for self-indulgence. We use our freedom to love our neighbors as ourselves.

Following the Shepherd may be more difficult today because we have to search for the Shepherd in a crowded spiritual marketplace. There is a virtual smorgasbord of Christian denominations and thousands of congregations from which to choose. No longer do you simply go to the church closest to your home. At times it is a bit bewildering to have so many styles of worship available to us. Anything from a silent Quaker service to energetic worship bands can be found on Sunday mornings. In the midst of the cacophony of spiritual sounds stands the same gentle Shepherd guiding us to truth.

It is easy to lose sight of the Good Shepherd and focus instead on the buildings or features of the individual congregation. The Shepherd invites us to turn away from spiritual invention, from people with high profile and low integrity, from the noise and frenzy of hyperactive addiction to emotion and focus on his central messages and turn to the one true voice.

The Individual Search

Following the Good Shepherd is foremost a matter of individual choice and commitment. The spiritual path may have other people on the same journey but the steps taken are always our own. As the African-American spiritual puts it, "You have to walk it by yourself." It is in the discipline of making room for Jesus that we give God the opportunity to bless us with spiritual gifts and moments of assurance.

There are countless resources, spiritual directors, pastors, and retreats to encourage our faith development. God does not set limits for our spiritual growth. We limit our faith by choosing the wrong priorities. Jesus sits at the watering hole waiting for us to come to drink. Songwriter Gloria Gaither invites the "Gentle Shepherd" to "come and lead us, for we need you to help us find the way."

Perhaps it is only when we turn down our boom boxes and moments of frenzy that we meet God. Maybe this is why the movement to Christian spiritual contemplation has flourished recently. Some Christians are reviving methods from earlier centuries that invite people to contemplative prayer as a way of being present with God. Jesus modeled taking time to be present with God in silence, prayer, the reading of Scripture, and contemplation. This centering prepared him for preaching, teaching, healing, and conflictual situations. Jesus understood that time alone with God was essential for an outer ministry.

The late Cardinal Bernadin of Chicago said that he tried to be inside with his outsides and outside with his insides. Our inner spiritual life and our outer Christian life must feed and maintain one another. It requires a meshing of faith and action. It looks for new and old rituals to express our understanding of God.

The Family Search

Perhaps family is the living gospel. Caring for loved ones is extending God's love. Allowing family to care for you is like taking a nap in the lap of God. The give-and-take in family life is part of the wonderful mystery of the Divine. Children can see a glimpse of God through their parents. Parents can model the spirit of gentleness and a transcendent God who is always nearby and dependable. Sheep really do count on a shepherd to be with them.

The shepherd's staff is used to steer and rescue the sheep, not to punish. Parents are responsible to lead their children and convey to them that fences are a necessary part of life. If children perceive that the fences are for their well-being and protection and not an opportunity to abuse power, they will see their parents as gentle shepherds and not arbitrary fence builders.

It is unfortunate in our day that "parents are no longer rule givers but rule breakers. It is up to the children to improvise a set of rules" (Whitehead, *The Divorce Culture*, Alfred A. Knopf, p. 125). It is hard to explain boundaries to children when parents divorce; have affairs; make poor financial decisions; and are violent, dishonest, and selfish. Authority is lost when the rule makers cannot govern their own lives. When parents are rule keepers, the fences they build for themselves and their children will provide plenty of room for exploring. These fences will also help to keep parents from getting lost.

Just as children can learn to know God through their

parents, parents can also experience God through their children. Why else would Jesus have said, "Let the children come to me, for the Kingdom of God belongs to such as they" (Mark 10:14, TLB). When a parent looks into the eyes of a child, it is a glimpse of heaven, or when that child is asleep, the peaceable kingdom. Children teach us to appreciate the sacredness of life. When have you last jumped in puddles while cheering for a magnificent rainbow? When have you played peekaboo with the moon? When have you chased fireflies and marveled over their lights? When have you last cried when your pet turtle died? Most likely a child led you in these moments of spontaneous worship of our Creator.

We can be families who are devoted to knowing God and not just families who "do" family devotions. We can pass on faith during the teachable moments of life: watching a sunset, observing birds, returning extra change given at the grocery store, lending a steady hand to an older person, saying we are sorry when we fail.

There are everyday opportunities to disciple our children. We can recite a psalm, sing a hymn, or offer a prayer that relates to the event we have just encountered. Some adults have reacted negatively to the tradition of daily family Bible reading and have chosen instead to let their children learn by example. Children do benefit highly from regular Bible reading, singing, and prayer. It may seem difficult in this fast-paced world to fit in family worship, but the family is still the most intimate unit on earth for experiencing God.

Families can also benefit from a theology of practice that defines what we believe. God instructed the children of Israel in Deuteronomy 6 to write their core commandments on their doorposts, mantels, and foreheads. They were to recite the commandments when sitting down, standing up, or walking. We may want to develop written mission statements to identify our core beliefs. This theology will include fence building that outlines boundaries for behavior as well as practices for spiritual growth. "It is the mission of Christians to preserve these basic spiritual values and to pass them on from generation to generation" (Muto, *Pathways of Spiritual Living*, St. Bede's Publishing, p. 26).

The Congregational Search

The congregation is a vital place to experience God in the company of others. God's people have always gathered to worship whether it was the children of Israel in the temple, the early Christian churches gathering in homes, or the early Anabaptists in the caves of Switzerland. It is in the gathering of the people that God is revealed in ways different from individual worship.

God's presence is made known in the hymns, the preaching, the reading of the Scripture, the moments of sharing, the prayers, and even in the announcements. We are assured that God is in our midst. It is one of the reasons it is so important to be there in person. Individual prayer is not enough and neither is television worship. The mystery of assembly cannot be created in any other way.

God is also revealed through the fellowship and nurturance of church members. It is a group to which we can belong and feel acceptance. It is like extended family. It is interesting to observe fellowship patterns by seeing how long members linger in the church foyer or on the steps after the church service is over.

Can one conclude that in these congregations where the most lingering takes place their members care more for each other? It would certainly suggest that the gathering is for both vertical and horizontal reasons. It is in that context that joys, hurts, and the common events are shared. God is a people person. We are invited to be God's hands and feet when our sisters and brothers are in need of care. Even though we may have sung the song one too many times, the words "and they'll know we are Christians by our love" still hold true.

Christians are called to service. No one can be a part of a Christian community and ignore the needs of our world. The call of the New Testament is to both faith and works. Offering the cup of cold water to a stranger who is thirsty is not an option. It is a requirement.

The congregation can be the context out of which service takes place. It can identify needs and provide the encouragement for service both local and abroad. There are endless opportunities. Churches are housing the homeless, offering soup kitchens, helping with Habitat for Humanity, tutoring students and newer immigrants, and running summer Bible schools. Our communities need us and we need them. As we serve, we often find that we have received much more than we have given.

The gathering of God's people is also to discern the truth from Scripture and of God who is newly revealed for our day. It is through the teaching from the leaders and the common insight of the gathered community that we form doctrine and practice.

In contrast to the old system that was authoritarian and top-down in edicts, today the membership participates in discernment. Individuals look to the local congregation and to the broader Christian community for guidance in their own lives. While it is unreasonable to think that all members will practice their faith identically, there can be some common standards.

Congregations work together to create fences. If guidance for lifestyle does not come from the church, individuals are left to make their own decisions. In a day in which the secular community promotes lifestyles with few limitations, the church can help to define morality and ethics. Fences on behavior are created and upheld by the church community. When mistakes are made, that same community can provide forgiveness. Whenever members are unwilling to receive counsel from the community, they become vulnerable to making serious errors.

Granted, there are vast differences in the interpretation of Scripture. At times these cause deep division and pain. Many church splits have happened when differences could not be negotiated. The church is an imperfect place. However most of the time it attempts to be faithful to Scripture while caring for its members. It is within this imperfect yet dynamic interplay that people who are guided by the gentle Shepherd build freedom fences.

The Goodness of Guilt

As important as the moral community is for guidance, the individual conscience remains a vital component for directing behavior. The conscience serves as a compass for decision making. Without it, community fences are never high enough to influence the choices people make. Each person stands or falls on the basis of how well the conscience works.

The conscience is a wonderful gift that prevents people from destructiveness. The conscience creates guilt when people go beyond morality fences. It is a pit-in-the-stomach feeling. It causes sleepless nights. It is the feeling of being separated from the offended people. These feelings can be effective correctives to carelessness. An invitation to gentleness: whether to God, others, or to self. Guilt, while unpleasant, can be a lifesaver. It can create intimacy. It can be a civilizing emotion.

While guilt may be handled differently by different cultures, it serves as a mediating influence in society. A guiltless society would be one of chaos. Even though some sectors of North America have tried to minimize guilt, the effects have often been negative. Teen pregnancies, drug abuse, violent acts, affairs, and divorce have increased dramatically during this period.

As Christians, we strive to be so close to the Shepherd that straying away from God's love is not our pattern. God is calling us home with guilt, not giving us a tongue-lashing. At times we will need guilt to prompt us to change our hearts or behavior. It is with the help of a conscience that God is able to speak to the soul. We are God's beloved sons and daughters, and God desires to keep us close.

That is not to say that guilt is always properly understood or correctly applied. Some people obsess over what they believe is wrongdoing. They feel emotional pain thinking they are bad people because of things they have done and feel out of harmony with God. No amount of confession or agony will fix the problem. They are not experiencing guilt the way God intended. It is not the kind of stirrings of conscience that can lead to a correction. Instead what feels like guilt becomes a prison from which they can never escape. Never, that is, until they recognize that it is not guilt at all. Instead, this feeling is from an emotional condition like depression or obsessive compulsiveness. Often this condition is medical, not spiritual. A good gauge of whether it is helpful guilt is to follow the words of Thomas Oden in *Guilt Free:* "One can only be guilty over that for which one is first responsible."

Some parents and churches have been overly strict and have shamed people into obedience rather than inviting members to faithfulness. They have based their definition of "goodness" upon following all of the right rules. Many of them are arbitrary. That kind of fence keeping distorts the purpose of conscience. If the law is consistently placed above love, it may not be a safe place for one to remain. It can create feelings of anger and worthlessness from which some people have a difficult time escaping.

Confession and Forgiveness

Our behavior offends others from time to time. We do injurious things. We separate from God. When the conscience works properly, it prods us to do something to correct the situation. Unexpressed guilt is as damaging as unexpressed grief. Or any other emotion. Going to a third party, even to a therapist, to talk it out does not completely resolve the problem. Other people cannot absolve us for a wrong we have done to someone else or fix our separation from God.

Guilt needs confession. If the offense was to a person, it requires an apology to that person. If it was to the broader community, to that community. Because it is always an offense to God, then a confession to God. Some people depend upon liturgical confession to wipe the slate clean. Many churches include group confession in the weekly worship service or songs that express regret for sinfulness. People confess their wrongdoing to God directly in prayer.

Many people have painful memories of revival-meeting confessions. Expressions that were spurred on by emotional sermons or by coercion. Testimony meetings were held in which individuals gave dramatic accounts of their encounters with wrongdoing and their attempts to make it right. Other people have memories of public confessions that were required for members who stepped outside the line. In some ways, these forms of confession seemed contrived, arbitrary, and punitive.

If guilt is to have its proper expression, there needs to be some form of public accountability. James 5:16 (NRSV) says, "Confess your sins to one another, and pray for one another, so that you may be healed." Litanies and songs are a form of confession but lack the personal responsibility which comes from the offender and the offended meeting each other for forgiveness and healing. Even whole congregations need healing. We may need new formats that are based more on the needs of the offender than those who want to punish. Guilt is the emotion that can lead to confession and from confession to reconciliation and healing.

Just as it is the responsibility of the offender to confess, it is also the responsibility of the offended to forgive. The deepest level of healing will not happen for either party unless that takes place. "When you refuse to forgive someone, you still want something from that person; even if it is revenge that you want, it keeps you tied to that person forever" (Townsend and Cloud, *Boundaries*, Zondervan Publishing, p. 134). People who live in unforgiveness deprive themselves of freedom. The gentle Shepherd leads us on the path to healing and grace.

Our goal is to be more spiritual individuals, families, and churches who are led by the gentle Shepherd. We are called to freedom in Christ. Freedom in Christ grows out of God's redeeming grace expressed in covenant. Let us choose to be surrounded by fences that come from personal decisions, together with our families and our congregations.

Freedom Fences

1. We will be active members of a local congregation with which we are compatible. We will

attend worship services regularly as well as participate in the programs of the congregation. We will support the congregation with our money and prayers and refrain from unnecessary criticism while working to improve weaknesses in the church.

2. We will raise our children with the expectation that they will make a commitment to Christ when they become accountable for their choices.

3. We will find creative ways to teach God's story to our children and pass on the faith. Nor accepting biblical illiteracy as the standard for our home. We will engage in learning as a family, knowing that the best learning happens cooperatively and interactively.

4. We will teach and model experiencing God through silence and reflective prayer. Let us offer an alternative to the noises coming from the world around us and even the hyperactivity within the Christian community.

5. We will be comfortable with the celebrations that can come from experiencing God as a rushing wind.

6. Because faith and service cannot be separated, let us live all of life in a spirit of service. We will find ways to reach out to our neighbors both near and far.

7. We will work as a family to build fences of freedom and to support each other in respecting

these fences. While the leadership for the fence building comes from the parents, it is imperative to involve the children in the decision making.

Questions

1. Why do some people have more trouble staying within fences than others?
2. How can you be sure that fences are not just the hang-up of some leaders?
3. Why can I not rely only on myself to be the best judge of right and wrong?
4. If I do not have any respect for my pastor, how can I listen to the sermons and receive direction?
5. I cannot find a congregation with which I am compatible. Where can I turn to search for a Christian community that will feed and nurture me?
6. I believe my guilt is a result of frightening sermons. How can I know the source of my guilt?
7. My children do not want to do any fence building. What are some things I can do to change their attitude?
8. How can my family find new ways to learn about God?

Activity

The children of Israel nailed their core beliefs to their doorposts. Identify your core beliefs and post them on your refrigerator. Refer to them. Pray about them. Teach them to your children.

Bibliography

Allen, David
1993 *In Search of the Heart*. Nashville: Thomas Nelson Publishers.

Berends, Polly Berrien
1991 *Gently Lead: How to Teach Your Children About God While Finding Out for Yourself*. New York: Harper Collins Publishers, Inc.

Cole, Robert
1990 *The Spiritual Life of Children*. Boston: Houghton Mifflin Co.

Johnson, Greg
1995 *What Would You Do If? 101 Five-Minute Devotions for the Family*. Ann Arbor: Servant Publications.

Kushner, Harold
1996 *How Good Do We Have to Be?* Boston: Little, Brown & Co.
Muto, Susan
1984 *Pathways of Spiritual Living*. Petersham: St. Bebes Publishing.
Oden, Thomas
1980 *Guilt Free*. Nashville: Abingdon.
Shenk, Sara Wenger
1987 *Why Not Celebrate!* Intercourse: Good Books.
Townsend, John, and Henry Cloud
1992 *Boundaries*. Grand Rapids: Zondervan Publishing.
Twitchell, James B.
1997 *For Shame: The Loss of Common Decency in American Culture*. New York: St. Martin's Press.
Whitehead, Barbara Defoe
1996 *The Divorce Culture*. New York: Alfred A. Knopf.

9

Children: Birth to Kindergarten

Train children in the right way, and when old, they will not stray. Proverbs 22:6 (NRSV)

Jesus . . . said to them, "Let the little children come to me; do not stop them; for it is to such as these that the kingdom of God belongs." . . . And he took them up in his arms, laid his hands on them, and blessed them. Mark 10:14, 16 (NRSV)

Parenting as a Calling

When adults become parents, they are given a wonderful gift and an awesome responsibility. Jesus clearly recognized the specialness of children by taking time to hold them and to bless them. Children had a place in his heart. They were his kingdom people. He did not push them away because he had more important things to do. He could have seen them after he came home from work. After all, he had some fishing to do, a medical clinic to run, and a donkey to catch to Nazareth where he had a big meeting coming up. Surely he could have found someone in the crowd to entertain them. Instead, Jesus welcomed them because he valued them. Perhaps in part because they were so powerless. So vulnerable.

So receptive to truth. They had not yet been spoiled by the follies of adulthood.

When we as parents welcome children onto our laps, is it with the same spirit that Jesus had? Would we cancel meetings for them? Do we give them special blessings? Do we go fishing, golfing, or catch the next plane for our big meetings? The choices are tough. Maybe tougher for us than for Jesus because life today is so much more hectic.

We soothe our consciences by offering a few minutes per day of "quality time" to children who, we believe, should be impressed. In case they miss the message, we buy them the latest gadgets and playthings. But Proverbs 22:6 does not let us off so easily. We are given the responsibility to train our children. Their adult choices will depend on what we taught them when they were children. It is hard to teach on the run. On marginal time. If other things are more important to us than our children, our words will seem empty. Children will get the real message.

Parenting as a Choice

The past several generations have been the first to be able to plan their families. Advances in birth control technology have been spurred on by concerns over worldwide population growth, changes in attitudes about sexual freedom, the wish to limit family size for economic reasons, and by the desire of women to have careers outside the home.

If preventing pregnancy has been made easy, other decisions about having children have not. A generation ago, couples may have chosen to limit family size, but they married younger and had their children earlier. Today many couples are concerned about material comforts and want to advance in their careers before starting their families. Some feel the first pressure to have children when their peers begin having babies or because of their concern with the decline in fertility rates as women age. When some have difficulty getting pregnant, they can feel resentful. Even guilty. Many resort to expensive medical treatments to solve the problem.

Couples who did not postpone having children but have been unable to conceive experience a variety of emotions. Some feel abandoned by God. Even resentful of peers who have children. They experience grief over their loss, and some blame each other. When treatment measures fail, many want to adopt children.

Many couples seek to be logical about an illogical decision—having children. There is no right time, right number, and right mix of genders. There will never be enough money in the bank or the right time to interrupt a career. It is impossible to take the unknown out of being a parent. It is the mystery of being parents that makes it special.

Parenting as a Gift

Many parents are delighted with their role and take their responsibilities seriously. In spite of the pressures and frustrations children can bring, the cost-to-benefit ratio still favors having children! Children expand their parents' horizons, teach them the blessings of sacrifices, and give them meaningful futures. Most parents become excited about giving shape to a moldable being. They experience the unconditional love of a child through the bonding that takes place from the moment of birth. In the eyes of a child, parents can see the goodness of God just as Jesus saw the kingdom of God in the children to whom he related.

Fathers and mothers are equally parents. Equal in

importance. Equal in responsibility. Equal in concern for the children. Usually one parent meets more of the daily needs of the child. However, the role of the other parent remains vital. When secondary parents allow their roles to be diminished by work or hobbies, everyone loses. It is important for fathers and mothers to work as teams. Children need to see them working together as a unit.

Our daughter Nina refers to a brief time when she and her husband, Craig, were doing what she calls "tag-team parenting." When one came home, the other went off to work, to a committee meeting, for recreation, or just to get a break. After a period of time, they chose to make changes because they wanted their children to experience them as coparents, not as shift workers coming on duty. This period of time in a child's life requires special energy and commitment from both parents.

Young Children and Dependency

Nobody ever said parenting would be easy. It is probably the toughest job most people will do in a lifetime. Partly because the job is never over. Partly because young children present unique challenges for parents. During this period their physical and emotional dependency upon their parents is at its greatest. Fortunately this dependency tapers off as children get older. But there is always work to be done: bathing, dressing, feeding, holding, diapering, and other tasks. These activities take time and use up a lot of parental energy.

Meeting the emotional needs of children is also demanding. As they move out of infancy, these needs become more intense. The parent is there to model, comfort, structure, answer questions, and provide a primary relationship to a developing child. In a sense, the emotional tasks are more complicated because they are not as clearly defined as the physical ones. A bath is a bath. There are not too many ways to do it.

Making the bath a meaningful time of bonding takes more skill. It is one thing to see the bath as an activity to clean the child's body. It is quite another responsibility for a parent to use the bath to convey love, caring, and to communicate. When parents respond to the child's physical and emotional needs, children feel valued and satisfied. Contented children are easier to care for and are being prepared for the independence that is coming.

Beginning the Journey to Independence

During this period a child begins the journey from dependence to independence. A brief journey that begins with an utterly dependent infant and ends with an emerging self-reliant child stepping onto the school bus for the first day of kindergarten. That step has enormous importance. It is one of many. In some ways it seems to come too soon.

But most children have an inner drive to become independent. Most of them are developing opinions about how to brush their teeth, which books to read, what foods they like, and other things. The irrepressible drive to learn and become competent is what motivates them. The moving on in life began at conception. It is a one-way journey. Some parents may try to slow down the process, but not for long. Childhood is mainly about growth and change. It is about moving from dependence to independence. It is also about innocence and mystery. Parents are there to enjoy and assist the process.

Parents Have Their Own Limits

Parents do not have to be perfect to be effective. Many are tired and frustrated. Parenting very young children takes time and is hard work. Nighttime feedings, unpredictable schedules, and crying babies who cannot adequately explain themselves take their toll. Young children have needs and sometimes unreasonable demands. It is hard for parents to make sense of it all and harder still to remain patient without adequate sleep.

Besides, most parents have other things to do like earning money, housecleaning, laundry, and mowing the yard. It can be hard to find time for the essentials like taking a shower. It may be impossible to do the extras like going out to dinner or reading a newspaper.

For some parents the job is particularly difficult because they did not get their needs met when they were growing up. They were not loved or given special blessings. It is hard to share something with a child that the parents were not given themselves. These parents often feel emotional emptiness. They might not have had adequate role models who taught them parenting skills. Some parents struggle with depression and feelings of inadequacy or have other medical problems that make parenting more difficult. Some mothers experience depression after delivery.

Other parents have trouble giving to their children because they were indulged and overprotected as children. They frequently want to be taken care of themselves and can find the needs of children too overwhelming. In spite of these influences, parents can do well. They can learn to pace themselves. To ask for help. To read and attend seminars or parent-support groups. The task is daunting. Even parents with personal limitations can learn to become better parents. It is also reassuring to know that many children are remarkably forgiving and flexible. Parents do not have to be perfect.

Special Challenges with Young Children

One of the things that makes parenting so difficult is that children are all different. What works for one does not work for the next. Some are quiet and some are loud. Some with high energy and some quite passive. It is so puzzling that they have the same parents and can be so different. Some children match up better with the personality of one parent than the other.

It is helpful when parents understand the unique personality of the child and make adjustments in their approach to meet the needs of that child. Parents who expect a "cookie cutter" approach to children will be disappointed. The children will be frustrated. Individual personalities require individual responses from parents. It makes the job harder but much more interesting and successful.

Some children have unusual needs. Special challenges come from children who are high energy, oppositional, dependent, or disorganized. They require extraordinary attention from parents. Some may have problems that require the assistance of physicians and child specialists. Increasing numbers of children are being diagnosed with attention deficit hyperactivity disorder. Many are placed on medication. While most of them are already in school when the condition is diagnosed, the symptoms are often present in the home for some time earlier. Children with these disorders may cause parents to lose their patience. They create extra stress in the home. Special steps can be taken to help them.

Some children are born with genetic and or other congenital impairments. These include Down's syndrome, sight and hearing impairments, cerebral palsy, spina bifida, and other kinds of challenges. Parents not only struggle with their grief from these impairments, but with the reality that these children will require extra care throughout life. Many parents compensate well and are creative in helping their children reach their highest potential. It is always a challenge that requires parents to work as a team and to find support from others, including families in similar situations.

The Spirited Child

Many parents are challenged by children who are high in energy and emotion. Some people refer to these children as strong-willed. Others may even call them hyperactive. Another view is that they are spirited. "They are normal children who are more intense, sensitive, perceptive, and uncomfortable with change than other children" (Kurcinka, *Raising Your Spirited Child,* Harper Collins, p. 7). Some of these children get overly stimulated in a crowd while others are intimidated. Birthday parties might be a disaster for them. These children are aware of very small intrusions into their lives, such as the labels on their shirt collars or wrinkled socks inside their shoes.

It is important for parents to understand spirited children because pressuring them or punishing them can even make the situation worse. Often parents of spirited children discover they have many of the same characteristics themselves. The goal is not to change the child's temperament but to "help the child understand his temperament, emphasize the strengths, and provide guidance he needs to express himself appropriately" (Kurcinka, p. 26).

Parenting and Finances

Children cost money. Depending on the spending habits of parents, lots of money. Houses are needed that provide enough space for them. The choice of vehicles is usually shaped by children. They use diapers by the truckload. Not to mention clothing for their changing sizes. Doctor bills increase. The child-product industry stands waiting in the hallway with an array of equipment no one would want to be without. These are the expenses that are hard to avoid. There are also expenses for the nonessentials. Toys, stuffed animals, rattles, and mobiles can fill an entire room. No well-equipped couple could enter parenting without a video camera! If the child is in daycare, more money is needed.

For the most part, parents do these things for their children because they are necessary. Children need space and equipment that is safe and most of the gadgets that entertain them. Few parents would want to go back to cloth diapers. The problem for parents is to decide what is excessive. When are they just being competitive with neighbors or family members? When have they allowed slick advertising to convince them to buy products they do not need? It is important for couples to be conservative with their spending urges.

It is exhilarating to have children, especially the first child! The adrenaline surge from becoming a parent can lead to unnecessary purchases. Yard sales can be a good way to contain costs. So can creating a budget before the first child is born. An unfortunate result of extra spending for some parents is that they both have to work to support their lifestyle. Would it not be better to live with less and have more time together as a family?

Parenting and Career

For many women, having children means their careers will be impacted. It may mean reducing the hours they work or placing their careers on hold. Women who return to work after maternity leave may meet resistance when they refuse overtime work, are selective in their work hours, or take time off for sick children. While some employers are tolerant of these limitations, many are not. Working mothers are still expected to be more responsible for children than working fathers, and many feel caught between the workplace and home.

Some women choose to interrupt their careers for part or all of the years their children are at home. Many find it rewarding to have consecutive careers at work and home. That is, they begin with careers outside the home, stop to raise children, and then return to careers. Attempting to maintain concurrent careers of parenting and working outside the home may result in neither being fully satisfying.

While their numbers are few, more fathers are choosing full-time parenting as a career. They can be very effective primary parents. Fathers who choose to continue their careers outside the home need to share parenting responsibilities in the evenings and on weekends. They too can pick up sick children at school, take children to the orthodontist, and do many other tasks that have traditionally been done by mothers. Parents are most effective when they raise their children as a team. They both have unique gifts to offer their children.

It is important to recognize that parenting careers last for a short time while outside careers can take up most of the adult years. Raising children successfully can enhance other career. In a culture that emphasizes the right to have everything now, parents are faced with difficult dilemmas. Are their careers the most important parts of their lives now or can they set careers aside for a season of parenting? Should their other outside involvements in hobbies, committees, and friendships be reduced during these critical years for children? Do all of these things have to happen now? It is a time of difficult choices.

Free Time

First-time parents will discover that having enough time for everything comes down to simple arithmetic. You add a child. You subtract some meetings or rounds of golf. Something. There simply is not enough time to do it all. It is clear that sacrifices are necessary. Becoming parents forces people to evaluate their priorities.

With creative time management, it is possible to preserve individual time for reflection and for some recreation. Some things can be done after children are in bed. Times for talking and for sexual intimacy may need to be planned. These moments can still have meaning. It is possible to meet the needs of children and still meet personal needs. But it will not happen without a plan for the creative use of time.

Changes in Lifestyle

Parents make sacrifices in some aspects of their lifestyle when they have children. The carpet takes on the color of the latest jelly. Walls constantly have smudges. The parent's clothing has to be inspected to make sure Cheerios are not accessories to the outfit. The van is not a sports car. Vacations are no longer exotic. Parties are for children's birthdays, and the guests are noisy kids.

While children create a new social environment, most parents adjust to the changes. They even come to like it. The lifestyle with children tends to be authentic. Only children get adults to crawl around on the floor and act silly. Regression is not only acceptable; it is necessary and wonderful.

Children stretch parents in other ways. Some parents rediscover bicycling. Although with a small passenger riding on a seat. It is still exercise. So is giving children a ride with the running stroller. Some discover new hobbies like guitar playing, play dough sculpting, or face painting. Some take up gardening with their children.

When parents get impatient with this stage of a child's life, they can be comforted in knowing that it will soon end. That it is only for a season and a surprisingly short season at that. When it is over, some parents have nostalgic urges to catch fireflies again or to throw a ball. These precious moments of epiphany and joy have a way of lodging deep in the soul of a parent.

Preventive Discipline

The primary goal of discipline is to teach children appropriate behavior. It is one of the main tasks of parents. Just as children need to be taught how to speak, walk, and manage their bowels and bladders, they also need to learn how to behave. It is an acquired skill. No child is born with a ready-made sense of how to act. The verse in Proverbs 22 encourages parents to "train children in the right way." That means teaching children about boundaries, about right and wrong, and about natural consequences. This is the time when the conscience begins to form.

Parents erect age-appropriate fences and explain to children why the fences are there. Fences for the time to go to bed and when to eat. It is important to teach children to share toys, not to bite, and not to throw food. Parents are teachers of the social code and of the behaviors that will make it possible to do well in a social world. Freedom without fences has never benefited a child. When children have no structure, they are overcome by their own power. It isolates them from peers and brings them into conflict with the adult world.

Changes in Discipline Styles

In several generations, we have gone from rigid parenting that depended upon punishment to parenting that is more laissez faire. From discipline as spanking to discipline as dialogue. From a long list of things children should not do to a short list of things that are to be "talked through."

Primary concern is now given to the self-esteem of children and to their right to make decisions for themselves. At the same time, the number of families with both parents working outside the home is increasing. Many children are learning discipline in group settings and from adults other than their parents. Boundaries for these children are less clear, and opportunities for doing preventive discipline are decreased.

Anticipating Needs

The best discipline is that which prevents trouble from happening in the first place. Discipline that anticipates problems ahead of time and meets needs before they surface through negative behavior. In an ideal world, all discipline would be preventive. In the real world, much more could be prevented. We cannot be preventive in our discipline without a plan and without being intentional. The energy of children is boundless. Their curiosity is endless, and their ability to make good judgments limited.

It is helpful when parents are a step ahead of the children and anticipate when the energy might become out of control. When parents miss the cues, they use much of their time and energy correcting or punishing. Punishment is often the end result of failed discipline—the moment when the parent loses control and exerts power. While parents may believe they are showing strength, inevitably children will see it as weakness, and the real problem will not be solved.

Discipline for Parents

We prevent discipline failures with our children, first of all, by being disciplined ourselves. That means we are comfortable with boundaries for our own lives. We know when to go to bed. How much to eat. We contain our work and recreation. We do not take on more assignments than we can handle. We become skillful at critical thinking and making decisions that do not bring harm to ourselves or others.

People who do preventive discipline have schedules. The schedules may have a flexible orderliness. The kind of orderliness that is comforting to children. Too many families live on the edge of chaos and have a hard time seeing the connection to their children's behavior. When parents choose disorder in their own lives, they lose the opportunity for preventive discipline. Instead they use their energy picking up the pieces from their own failures that surface in their children's behavior.

Stories

I once observed a three-year-old boy trying to get the attention of his father who was reading the newspaper. The child made numerous verbal requests to the father that were ignored. After several minutes the child resorted to violence. He knocked the paper out of the father's hands. The father responded with violence by spanking the child. This interchange between father and son could have been avoided. Preventive discipline would have worked if the father had first volunteered to read the book to his son or spent time playing with him before he read the newspaper. When we neglect our preventive responsibilities, the child and the parent pay an unnecessary price.

At another time I came upon a mother in the grocery store with a young daughter in the seat of the grocery cart. It was obviously mealtime. As the mother and daughter passed the cereal aisle, a battle began over the child's wish for a certain kind of cereal. At first the mother tried bargaining, even talking about how the daughter was feeling about the cereal. Several aisles later the debate was still going on and getting louder. The mother removed the daughter from the cart and took her outside where she severely reprimanded her. Preventive discipline would have avoided shopping at mealtime. If that could not be avoided, she would have taken food along for the child. A preventive parent would have talked about cereal choices before leaving home to go shopping.

We heard of a couple who was having problems in their marriage. They were having too little time for each other. Arguments had become frequent. Intimate moments were becoming less frequent. Their six-year-old son and four-year-old daughter stayed up with them until eleven each night watching television. The son frequently had behavior problems in school, and the daughter argued with her mother. The family tensions were high. Preventive discipline would have meant turning off the television much earlier, dedicating time for reading to the children, and doing some satisfying activities with them. The children would have been in bed much earlier and would have felt better the next day. The parents would have had more time for each other.

Discipline: Corrective

The purpose of corrective discipline is to stop a child's inappropriate behavior. It happens when parents miss preventive opportunities. It should always be a secondary method. However, no parent is perfect, and it is important to find helpful ways to be corrective. Some children's personalities make corrective discipline more necessary. It is hard for them to control their impulses, even in a managed environment. The key to the success of the corrective discipline is for it to occur promptly after the misbehavior and for parents to be in control of their responses.

In his book, *1-2-3 Magic,* Thomas Phelan emphasizes that parents often fail with corrective discipline because they resort to using words too much and *they* lose control of their emotions. When parents fuss, children tune then out. They become immune to the words. When parents yell and threaten, children become reactive and increase their aggression. Bargaining, debating, and moralizing are not verbal tools which work well. Phelan believes that when parents lose control of their emotions they regress to the level of the child and lose their authority.

The appropriate corrective is for parents to express themselves clearly and with firmness. Parents can use a system of warnings and follow up with an action that intervenes with the inappropriate behavior. Children can spend time-out on chairs, rugs, or in their rooms as a way to interrupt offensive behavior. This gives the parents time to catch their breath and refocuses the child's behavior. These time-outs should be for short periods and appropriate to their age.

Taking away privileges or limiting an activity can be effective for some children. Some may respond to having their computer time or a special TV program restricted. As much as possible, the corrective discipline should relate to the inappropriate behavior. Natural consequences can be the best teacher. The goal of corrective discipline is to teach the child appropriate behavior. It is not a contest of wills between the parents and the children.

Freedom Fences

1. Just as Jesus welcomed the children onto his lap, parents will accept their responsibilities as the highest and most important calling. Nothing can exceed it in importance.

2. Parenting is most effective when it is done as equal partners by parents who make sacrifices for their children.

3. Preventive discipline of children begins with parents who are disciplined in their own lives.

4. Structured freedom for children is the most effective way for children to learn self-discipline. That includes reasonable routines and schedules as well as expectations for disciplined behavior.

5. Corrective discipline is never abusive and is only done to teach children a better way of behaving. When done correctly it replaces the need for punishment.

6. One of the goals of parenting is to help children begin their journeys toward independence and self-sufficiency. Giving children the special blessings of dedicated parenting is the first step in preparing them for adulthood.

7. In this season of parenting young children, mothers and fathers will know that even though the demands on their time and energy are at their greatest, relief is on the way. Children grow up. In the meantime parents will accept the responsibility to nurture children to the full measure required. There cannot be part-time parents.

Questions

1. In what ways is parenting a calling to you?
2. Why is quality time not good enough?
3. How can parenting be done equally when one spouse works outside the home?
4. What are the unique demands on parents when both work outside the home?
5. In what ways have your lives changed since you became parents?
6. Why is it not enough to just meet the physical needs of children?
7. Discuss ways you could change your family environment to practice preventive discipline.
8. What special problems come from personality differences between you and your children?

Activity

Plan Scrapbooks

Plan scrapbooks for your children. Give each child a scrapbook on his or her eighteenth birthday. What items would you like to include? What pictures of you should be there? What decisions can you make now to be sure those pictures will be included?

Bibliography

Brazelton, T. Berry

1992 *Touchpoints: Your Child's Emotional and Behavorial Development. The Essential Reference.* New York: Addison Wesley Publishing Co.

Brazelton, T. Berry, and Bertrand G. Cramer

1990 *The Earliest Relationship: Parents, Infants, and the Drama of Early Attachment*. New York: Addison Wesley Publishing Co.

Drescher, John

1988 *Seven Things Children Need*. Scottdale: Herald Press.

Elium, Jeanne and Don

1994 *Raising a Daughter: Parents and the Awakening of a Healthy Woman*. Berkley: Celestial Arts.

1996 *Raising a Son: Parents and the Making of a Healthy Man*. Berkley: Celestial Arts.

Eyre, Linda and Richard

1993 *Teaching Your Children Values*. New York: Simon & Schuster.

Faber, Adele and Elaine Mazlish

1987 *Siblings Without Rivalry: How to Help Your Children Live Together So You Can Live Too*. New York: Wade Publishers.

Ferber, Richard

1985 *Solve Your Child's Sleep Problems*. New York: Simon & Schuster.

Hallowell, Edward M., and John Ratey

1994 *Driven to Distraction: Recognizing and Coping with Attention Deficit Disorder from Childhood Through Adulthood*. New York: Banton Books.

Kurcinka, Mary Sheedy

1991 *Raising Your Spirited Child: A Guide for Parents Whose Child Is More Intense, Sensitive, Perceptive, Energetic*. New York: Harper Collins.

Phelan, Thomas
1995 *1-2-3 Magic.* Glen Ellgan: Child Management Inc.
Satter, Ellyn
1987 *How to Get Your Kid to Eat . . . But Not Too Much.* Palo Alto: Bull Publishing.
Tobias, Cynthia Ulrich
1994 *The Way They Learn: How to Discover and Teach to Your Child's Strengths.* Colorado Springs: Focus on the Family.

10

The Peaceful Years: Parenting for Middle Childhood

I will teach you the way that is good and right.
1 Samuel 12:23 (NIV)

My child, be attentive to my wisdom; incline your ear to my understanding, so that you may hold on to prudence, and your lips may guard knowledge. Proverbs 5:1-2 (NRSV)

Important Development

This period for children begins with that very large step onto the kindergarten bus. In a sense, this is the first step toward leaving home. The teacher becomes a substitute parent. The schoolmates become new siblings. The school building is a replacement for home. When children make this step, they are giving up some of their dependency and learning to become self-reliant. It is a process that will continue until they leave home for good in early adulthood. They have begun a one-way journey. The process is part emotional and part intellectual. Emotionally, children may be filled with sadness because of what they are giving up and because of their fear of the unknown. Children are also filled with the joy of anticipation and are irrepressibly curious. This part is intellectual. The wish to know and to discover begins young. They want to learn, and they know school is for that purpose.

Throughout this period children mature rapidly in their skills and their understanding of the world around them. They become competent, independent people who learn to do most things for themselves. They lean on their parents for less and less. For the most part, they transit through this stage peacefully. They may cause moments of discord but require much less attention from their parents than their younger siblings. They bring on far fewer headaches than their adolescent siblings.

Most parents look forward to having their children become more independent because they are ready to give up changing diapers, cleaning up messes under highchairs, and answering "why" questions. Even though the emerging young child may have opinions that differ from the parents, it is with a sense of relief to see that maturation is taking place. Parents are usually pleased that their children are growing up.

With the child's independence and power also comes activity. Lots of it. And most of it away from home. For many parents, these are the busiest years of child rearing. The years which invented "soccer moms." Children need to be taken to school activities. To sports events. To music lessons. To church programs. And to lots of places with their friends. Sleepovers become common. Many parents feel like taxi drivers and dispatchers. Family life is centered on the activities of children in these years.

The Social Language

This period is vital for learning the social code.

Children learn how to speak. That is, not just the words to use but the tone of voice and volume. The right way to walk, run, and play, and many other behaviors. There is a code which children need to learn. School is a living laboratory for social learning. The laboratory is the classroom, the playground, and the bus ride to and from school. It is in these settings where children get their social cues. Most children are adept and have an easy time fitting in. They have high social IQs. They learn the language quickly and use it skillfully.

Some children are not so lucky. For a variety of reasons, social learning comes harder. These children may be shy and passive. Some cannot read the social code. These children begin to drift away from the mainstream early in school. They are at the edge of the group or are excluded altogether. In a similar way, children who are overly aggressive are excluded by peers who feel threatened by them.

When the social learning process begins, many parents are unprepared for the changes they see in their children. The slang the children bring home. Sometimes it is the swagger learned on the playground. Most often it is an increase in aggression. Children return to the home with the adrenaline still flowing. They talk faster and louder. Their behavior has an edge. The innocence is gone. Parents must discern which new social skills to encourage and which to discourage.

Some parents resist these changes, but the changes are a necessary part of the child's maturation. It is a part of the child becoming confident and getting ready for living in a social world. Children who do not learn the social language will need encouragement by parents and teachers. The longer the deficiency continues, the harder it will be to change. Parents need to be involved early in making an assessment of their child's social progress. When any of the negative patterns are seen, corrective steps can be taken. Perhaps the problem will be resolved easily by inviting a friend to the house to strengthen social skills in a more manageable setting. Sometimes it requires that parents look for outside resources to help them understand the child's needs.

The Language of Education

School becomes important to children for intellectual learning. While they have been learning rapidly within the family, church, and other settings, school is a more structured setting. Although it is an environment that is intimidating in size, complexity, and expectations, it is the place where children learn the official language of education. Some do well, many do average, and some do poorly. Part of the challenge comes from the need to engage in a teaching/learning process that cannot be individualized for different personalities and different learning styles. Remarkably, most students achieve at least a degree of competence. "Kids don't need perfect classrooms that fit their temperament 100 percent of the time—just a majority of the time." (Kurcinka, *Raising Your Spirited Child*. Harper Collins p. 274) For school to work well, it is important for parents and teachers to work together to understand the needs of each child.

Students who learn unusually well in this system often feel frustrated by the slower pace of other students. Teachers and parents have to find other ways to challenge them. Socially, these students can feel rejection from their less successful peers who may feel inferior to them. In fact, some good students even slack off on their work to maintain friendships. On the other hand, some students equate self-worth with high grades. Often parents pressure them to succeed and make their approval based upon a good report card. The students who do best are those for whom learning is energizing. They have a passion for discovery. They are strong enough to deal with peer pressure and confident enough not to be affected by undue parental pressure.

Many average students are comfortable with the learning process even if it is only marginally interesting. They are not threatened by their peers who are faster learners and have no need to compete with them. These children often have other interests in which they excel. They are involved enough in school successes to make it worth their while. They often get more out of the social learning than the academic learning.

However, some students equate being average in the classroom with being less significant. They may get that message because schools focus more on the high and low achievers and the middle student gets left out. They may receive that idea from parents who believe that being average means being inferior. It is interesting to observe that some adults who have little self-confidence refer to their school years with the self-deprecating phrase, "I was only average." The emotion that accompanies the phrase is "therefore, I am not worth much." Being average needs a poster child! These children can benefit from receiving special blessings at school and home. They are the silent middle. Their needs are often overlooked.

Many of the children who do not fit well into the traditional classroom have learning problems associated with dyslexia, attention deficit disorder, hyperactivity, and impulse control. They present special challenges to both school and parents. Some respond to special teaching methods. Some receive help through guidance counselors. Some may need medication. However, parents have a vital part to play in finding answers for the needs of their children by making the changes in the home environment that will support the children's growth. That means the children will get proper sleep and nutrition. Parents will create an environment at home that limits distractions. Television, music, and computer games need to be controlled. Parents need to manage their own lives if their children are to learn to manage theirs.

Parents can contribute to their children's learning by setting up learning centers in their home and having learning times set aside each evening. It is important to establish the concept before the first child enters kindergarten. If a positive expectation for learning is a part of the family environment from the first day of school, problems can be prevented later. Learning is a structured activity that needs its own time and space. When it is done in the margins of family life, children often make marginal adjustments to learning.

The learning centers will be in a part of the house that is dedicated just to that purpose. Perhaps an unused room, a section of the basement that is fixed up for this purpose, or a sectioned-off part of a room that has other uses. However, the kitchen table or the family room have too many intrusions and are not conducive to learning. While the children's bedrooms may work for some, bedrooms can isolate children from the rest of the family.

Learning needs to be a family activity. During the established learning times, all family members should be engaged in an activity of learning; reading, doing hobbies, or catching up with financial management. The television and computer games need to be off and the environment quiet. Whether to have music playing in the background needs to be determined by whether it helps or hinders concentration. Small children may need to be cared for in another part of the house by one of the parents during study time. The other parent can be the monitor of the study period.

The Language of Work

During the middle childhood years, children learn to work. At first they do simple chores like putting their dirty clothes in the hamper or picking up toys. By the end of the period, they can do more complicated tasks like mowing the lawn or helping with kitchen cleanup. It may be difficult to find meaningful chores for children to do today, but children can play an important part in keeping a home running smoothly. Their assignments need to be appropriate for their age.

Attitudes formed about work during this period influence children later in their adult years. If chores are handled well now, work will most likely be a positive experience later. A part of developing maturity in work attitudes is doing tasks that themselves are unrewarding. What messages do parents convey about uninteresting, unpleasant, and tedious work? If these tasks are ignored, children will get the message that they can avoid work that they do not want to do. When parents complain, they teach negative attitudes about work.

Most often, it is helpful for parents and children to work together. It is unrealistic for parents to give assignments and expect children to complete the tasks themselves. As children get closer to adolescence, they may do better on their own, but most still need a parent nearby. Their attention spans are too short and their commitments are too small to complete tasks alone. Parent-child conflicts often happen because of the unrealistic expectations of parents. Working together with children can provide parents with good opportunities for building relationships. Some parents resist giving chores to their children because: (1) it is easier for the parents to do the work themselves, (2) they do not want to interfere with the children's play time, (3) they believe that the children will have the rest of their lives to work; or (4) the parents had bad experiences with chores when they were children. They may be ignoring the positive contribution chores can make to children and to family life.

Becoming Disciplined

Discipline during middle childhood is much different from the earlier years. It shifts from being parent-directed to becoming more child-directed. Many of the messages about behavior are already learned and internalized. The parent's role is changing. The children can be expected to brush their teeth, to dress themselves, and to take more responsibility for catching the bus. Parents still set the structures in place and are there to remind children of what is expected. Gradually children learn to manage more of their lives.

Preventive discipline is still important. Just as when the children were younger, parents need to live disciplined lives themselves. Parent chaos will generate child chaos. Parents who are too busy create children who feel neglected, become angry, and make mischief. Some of them escape into apathy.

Attentive parents will know their children well enough to anticipate problems and read the children's danger signs. They will also recognize when their children are having problems with peers, teachers, or with their schoolwork. The role of the parents in preventive discipline is to discover what is wrong before it develops into a larger problem. Parents who are attentive will help their children deal with the sources of their problems instead of dealing with the symptoms. Conflicts over television, showers, homework, or sibling squabbles are rarely the real problems. Often the problems are hidden behind the noise of battle. Only attentive parents will figure out the sources.

Because no parent is perfect, there will always be a need for corrective discipline. For some children, talking over the infractions may be enough to resolve the issues. Parents need to use care to state their case simply and straightforwardly. Long speeches never work. Neither will threats or debates. This is not a contest of peers. Parental strength comes from maturity and wisdom, not from a show of power that is based on physical strength or rank. The best kind of correction comes when parents and children work at understanding why certain behaviors are hurtful. Most of the time the children know it on their own but a gentle reminder from the parent confirms it.

In some instances children may need to have privileges taken away as an extra reminder of the mistake. It may be restricting the phone, television, computer, or even outside activities for a period of time. Often just spending time alone in their rooms provides time for reflection about the behavior. While parents may need to be very firm to make their point, physical or emotional punishment is rarely helpful. When violence is used as an effort to control behavior, it degrades the relationship and creates a whole set of other problems.

Morality, Values, and Sexuality

Just as the first stage of a child's life is important for the development of a conscience, a child at this stage begins to understand ethics and morality. The reasons things are right and wrong. The connections between what we do and the consequences of behavior. The days of innocence are over. The questions get tougher.

Children no longer accept the "do as I say, not as I do" edicts from parents. They have trouble dealing with inconsistency and hypocrisy.

Although children form their images of God through their parents during this stage, they can also understand imperfection. In the mistakes of their parents and their own, they learn the meaning of forgiveness. It is a model for knowing a forgiving God. It is also a time for understanding that choices have consequences, some of them serious. These years are important in developing a readiness to make the choice to become a Christian during adolescence.

It is also a time to expand their understanding of sexuality. Parents should not be concerned about giving lessons in anatomy. The school systems have assumed that role. They give more information than most young people want to hear. But public schools cannot place all of this information in a moral context. That assignment is left for parents and the churches.

Puberty may begin as early as nine or ten. Parents can prepare children for the changes and help them feel comfortable when the changes occur. Children receive mixed messages about male and female sexuality. "They will get the messages that girls are raised to value themselves as whole people but the media reduces them to bodies and that boys are encouraged to be sexy and sexual all the time" (Pipher, *Reviving Ophelia,* Ballantine Books, p. 206). We cannot totally protect children from these confusing messages, but we can influence how they will respond to them.

They can learn that character is more important than appearance or strength. Even young children know more about sex earlier than most parents did when they were young. Parents and church leaders can teach children about restraint and not having everything they want. Children can even begin to understand why sexual activity is reserved for marriage.

It is important that children feel comfortable with being male or female. They will want some privacy and that wish should be respected. This is the time for parents to be more careful in how they handle sexual intimacy and to be dressed modestly around the children. While it is important to convey a feeling of comfort about sexuality, it is also necessary for children to recognize that boundaries are important.

Expanding Interests and Activities

Middle childhood children invented the "soccer mom" to take them places. Many of these parents take time to watch them play soccer and baseball or sit in the bleachers to watch them learn gymnastics. Others transport children to piano lessons, to the boys and girls clubs at church, or to summer camps. Frequently trips are made to their friends' houses. Children of this age are busy. They have discovered that a big world exists outside their homes, and they do not want to miss the action. The activity is partly to meet social needs and partly to learn other skills that home life cannot offer. As inconvenient as it may be for parents, these kinds of activities are vital to the growth of children. Children need a mixture of organized and spontaneous activity.

When I was a young boy in the late 1940s, my friends and I used our free time building dams in the small creek that flowed through our hollow. We made trails in the hills behind our house where we would disappear for hours. We even played "war" in the meadow during the Korean conflict. One summer, a local coal baron believed that the boys of the hollow needed organized baseball. We barely had enough boys to make a team, but we felt important. We were a part of something bigger than ourselves. We had uniforms, new bats, gloves, and an official schedule that announced the dates and location for meeting the opponents from nearby mining villages. We were the first generation to be given this privilege. Our mothers took our pictures and kept the uniforms clean. But none of us had more than a passing thought of baseball stardom. Parents did not even come to our games. It was structured play with a hint of extravagance, but nothing more.

If children and parents keep things in perspective, organized activities can be positive. It is important for children of this age to belong to teams, develop skills, and even win some games. The structure that organized fun can bring is certainly better than sitting at home in front of the television. What child of this age would want to miss a team ride to the local Dairy Queen after the game? Sports really can be a metaphor for life. Before their children are seven or eight, most parents can teach the skills to their children just by playing with them in the backyard. There is nothing to be gained by starting children too early in organized sports.

The development of skills in music, gymnastics, art, and other areas has also increased markedly in recent years. Just as in competitive sports, it is important for children to discover and develop their interests. To stretch beyond their comfort zone and to be a part of something bigger than themselves.

When Activities Are Out of Balance

On the other hand, organized play can be taken too seriously. It seems excessive for very young children to be on sports teams. Winning the championship has become the ultimate achievement. Parents and coaches sometimes want the children to play each game like it is the Super Bowl. Players feel pressure to achieve at a high level. Statistics are kept on their accomplishments. Some with special talent are put on the fast track for high school teams, and parents begin dreaming of athletic scholarships that will pay their children's college education. Children are encouraged to be in sports each season, leaving them with little free time. Some of their tournaments are scheduled on Sunday morning or conflict with church camp. Family vacations are postponed or canceled altogether because of allegiance to the coach or to the team. Families need to decide how many activities children will be in and how much the activities will be permitted to control family life.

Unfortunately, these activities can belong more to coaches, recreation leaders, instructors, and specialty camps than they do to the children. These leaders promote the idea that they are building character, developing future athletes, and keeping children out of trouble. It is easy to convince parents of that. Especially if parents need the accomplishments of their children for their own self esteem. Most communities buy into the idea that one sport or another is more important than anything else. Pressure is placed on families and their children to enter these activities at a young age and to give large amounts of time to them.

Blue ribbons and trophies themselves do not make the child a better person. When competition becomes the main thing in children's lives, something very valuable is taken from them. Surely, some of the achievements have importance for adulthood. It is valuable for adults to play the piano well. However, if parents expect a child to become a concert pianist, that places too much pressure on the child. Learning a skill should have meaning in itself and should not be to benefit parents.

Children of this age cannot make decisions about activities that may be important to them in the future.

They tend to respond to their parents wishes and try to please them. Author David Elkind writes about a society that pressures children to grow up too quickly. This pressure "reflects the new attitude that the years of childhood are not to be frittered away by engaging in activities merely for fun. Rather, the years are to be used to perfect skills and abilities that are the same as those of adults" (*The Hurried Child,* Addison Wesley Publishing, p. 9).

Becoming Family

During this phase, children learn what it means to be family. They can no longer remain dependent infants and preschoolers who are taken care of by others. They are emerging as individuals in their own right, with their opinions and unique personalities and with the ability to think analytically about their families They have become voting members of a community. It may be within their power to choose McDonalds over Burger King, to have an opinion about what clothing to wear, or to know where to go on vacation. They are becoming fully certified people.

Children of this age are beginning to figure out where they fit in the pecking order And what happens during times of disagreements. How to give and take. Families become safe settings for learning how to act, think, and feel. Their view of the world is seen through the windows of their families.

In some ways, this period of relative calm is the most critical one in the preparation for adolescence. Children have not yet been overcome with the intense drive to separate from parents. In terms of teachable moments, this period is extraordinarily rich with many opportunities. According to author John Drescher, "middle childhood is especially crucial in the development of the inner life which prepares the child for the rest of life. Here the foundations are laid for the teen years" (*When Your Child Is 6 to 12*, Good Books, p. 7). It is in words of Samuel, a time for learning what is "good and right" (1 Sam. 12:23, NIV).

During these years, it is tempting for parents to relax and believe that their children no longer need them except for food and transportation. Parents are understandably relieved that the heaviness of the previous period of development is lifted from their shoulders. They welcome this time when their children require less maintenance. If children go through this stage successfully, it is a good sign for the stages that follow.

An important way to help children grow is through family rituals. Mary Pipher emphasizes that family rituals are important for relationship building. She says "making school lunches, tying shoes, walking the dog, doing the dishes—any act that's done with love becomes a ritual" (*The Shelter of Each Other*, Ballantine Books, p. 231-232). They also give children a sense of continuity and predictability. Rituals around holidays and birthdays create memories and expectations. The smell of the turkey at Thanksgiving, the trip to the tree farm at Christmas, and the cake for the birthday all create continuity.

Family rituals are established through vacations. They create legends that are retold for years to come. Vacations that allow for conversation during long rides to the next place. Campfires. Spectacular sights. Doing new things together as a family. The only way these things can happen is when the family is alone on vacation. No phones. No committee meetings. Vacations are islands of retreat in a sea of busy-ness. They create the memories that count for a lifetime. They make a positive statement about the importance of family. Sometimes the format is changed for special meaning. Fathers can take daughters on canoe trips. Mothers can take sons camping. Children are enriched when their boundaries are extended beyond the usual. Sometimes they may need to be stretched by parents who know that life is bigger than theme parks and boardwalks. The best vacations involve serendipity. Real fun cannot be manufactured.

Most of family life for children is lived in the ordinary. It is in that context that some of the richest legacies are built. Pizza every Friday night is legendary. So is feeding the ducks in the town park on Sunday afternoon. It is the stuff around which tradition is built. These are times for family bonding. Times for talking, for reflecting, for dreaming. If these things are not started now, it will be much more difficult to do them during the teen years.

Legacies also get built around family service projects. Balanced families share their emotional wealth with others. They reach out to people in need. They take time to clean streams or pick up trash along highways. Families need to get outside of themselves to be at peace within themselves. When parents feel comfortable with solitude, children will be more comfortable with quietness and activities which foster reflection. Families grow when they do readers' theater for residents in nursing homes or when they read for the blind. They grow when they mow yards or trim shrubs for people who are disabled. Some families are able to do volunteer work in communities in which there have been disasters. Family legacies are built through giving.

If these years are indeed peaceful compared to the other periods of parenting, it is partly because of the biology of the stage and partly because parents have done their job well. God seems to give parents a breather with children who are growing in their independence, but it is hardly a holiday. It is a time of extraordinary activity. Perhaps some of it excessive. Children of this age are busy exploring. The role of parents is to be actively engaged with their children during this critical time. Teaching. Modeling. Relating. Creating fences that are appropriate to the needs of children of this age. It is both a challenge and a privilege.

FREEDOM FENCES

1. Learn to know your children's friends and their parents. Welcome them into your home. Some friendships may need some boundaries.

2. Help your children cultivate friendships with other adults at church and in the extended family.

3. Establish two nights per week and Sundays as family times that will be protected from outside intrusions.

4. Before children begin taking part in organized activities, determine a limit for each child and a total limit for the family.

5. Discuss family rules for conduct at mealtime, manners, language, TV and computer use, and privacy.

6. Create a family learning center and a family learning time.

7. Develop positive attitudes about work through parent modeling and through parent

participation with children in chores.

8. Establish a family bond through meaningful rituals, vacations, and other activities that create a sense of cohesion and identity.

9. Model Christian integrity, boundary keeping, and forgiveness as a way of preparing children for adolescence.

Questions

1. With all the activity of these years, how can they be called peaceful?
2. If children are close to their parents, why is it important that they also have peer friends and other adult friends?
3. Teachers are paid to educate students. Why should parents be expected to help?
4. If a little pressure from parents helps students get straight A's, what is wrong with that? Why would anyone want to be average?
5. When I'm working around the house it takes longer if children help. Why can't they learn those skills later?
6. How can I know when my children are in too many activities and know which ones might have a long-term negative impact on them?
7. What's wrong with always going to a theme park for vacation? What are some other ideas for vacations?
8. I am uncomfortable talking about sex with my children. Why can't the church or the school do that for me?
9. How can I help my children have a healthy attitude

about sexuality and at the same time understand the importance of reserving sex for marriage?

Activity

Develop a family action plan with your children to balance: (1) family time, (2) outside activities, (3) friendships, (4) vacations, (5) rituals, (6) free time use, (7) work and chores, and (8) worship.

Bibliography

Bain, Lisa J.
1991 *Parent's Guide to Attention Deficit Disorders.* New York: Dell Publishing.

Drescher, John M.
1993 *When Your Child Is 6 to 12.* Intercourse: Good Books.

Elkind, David
1981 *The Hurried Child.* Reading: Addison Wesley Publishing Co.

Eyre, Linda and Richard
1993 *Teaching Your Children Values.* New York: Simon & Schuster.
1984 *Teaching Your Children Responsibility.* New York: Simon & Schuster.

Ingersoll, Barbara D., and Sam Goldstein
1994 *Attention Deficit Disorder and Learning Disabilities.* New York: Doubleday.

Kraehmer, Steffen T.
1994 *Quantity Time.* Minneapolis: Deaconess Press.

McGinnis, James and Kathleen
1990 *Parenting for Peace and Justice.* Maryknoll: Orbis Books.

Miller, Melissa A.
1994 *Family Violence.* Scottdale: Herald Press.

Pipher, Mary
1994 *Reviving Ophelia*. New York: Ballantine Books.
1996 *The Shelter of Each Other*. New York: Putnam Books.

Talley, Scott
1990 *Talking with Your Kids About the Birds and the Bees*. Ventura: Regal Books.

11

Adolescence: Searching for Independence

Mother: "Son, why have you treated us like this? Your father and I have been anxiously searching for you."
Son: "Why were you searching for me?"
The son offered an explanation, but they did not understand what he was saying to them.

I'm Okay. Why Aren't You?

This brief dialogue is between a parent and her adolescent son. If it sounds familiar, it may be because something similar has happened in your life. A son or daughter did not come home at the expected time. Teens told you they were going to be at one place and you eventually found them at another. These are moments of both fright and irritation for parents. For the adolescents, these are moments of being puzzled. They cannot understand why their parents are making a "big deal" out of such a little thing. "After all, Mom and Dad, I was all right and nothing bad happened." Parents and adolescents often have trouble understanding each other.

This dialogue may also sound familiar because it took place between Mary and Jesus after attending the Feast of the Passover. It is adapted from the account in Luke 2:41-52. For some reason, Mary and Joseph did not keep close tabs on their twelve-year-old son on their journey back to their home and did not discover that he was missing for about a day. Jesus was not up to mischief or in danger. He was listening to the teachers in the temple and asking them questions. Jesus knew where he was and that he was not doing anything wrong. So that should be enough. Jesus could not understand why his parents were upset. His response is typical for adolescents.

Jesus was emerging from underneath his parents' protective wings. He was beginning to think for himself and becoming independent. It is safe to assume that the family had attended Passover in the preceding years without incident. Then why this year? Could it have been his budding adolescence that gave him the drive toward independence? Even though he explained to his parents that he was doing God's work, there was obviously a communication gap developing between them. They were apparently not yet ready for these changes.

On the Path to Independence

Adolescence is about independence. About emergence into selfhood. About self-reliance. As much as parents may want to hold onto the comfort of the middle years of childhood, the growth hormones and the sex hormones say otherwise. The process was set in motion at the moment of conception. The transformation to adulthood is in the genetic program. The dilemma for parents is how to handle this newly developing adult.

As prepared as any parent might be, there is always an element of surprise. Every child becomes an adolescent differently. They seem to think of new ways to perplex their parents. Many parents are not prepared to surrender their children to independence. They hold on too tightly and create unnecessary problems for themselves and their children. Other parents have few structures in place. They get a rude awakening when their previously placid child becomes argumentative, aggressive, sexually driven, or disappears like Jesus did. Usually parents find their adolescents at their friends' houses, not in the temple, though. However, the emotions of parents today are similar to those of Jesus' parents. It is not easy being the parents of adolescents.

What Makes Teens Who They Are?

The hormones that are so necessary for adulthood are the very ones that can create problems in teens. The growth hormones make the body bigger and stimulate changes in the ways the body works, even in the ways the brain processes information. It is impossible to attain maturity without the hormone driven growth spurt. The sex hormones influence both physical and emotional changes. The development of sexual maturity in the reproductive systems, as well as secondary sexual characteristics that create sexual attraction, are brought about by the surge of hormones. The sex hormones create passion, arousal, and aggression. Adolescence is a physiological process that carry with them emotional, social, and spiritual implications.

The physically driven changes project children into adulthood much the way they were thrust into the world at birth. They have no choice. Physical adulthood is inevitable at birth. Fortunately this "second birth" is not as sudden as the first, and the child this time is much more aware of what is taking place. There is more openness today in discussing the changes that occur in youth. Teachers, parents, older cousins, or siblings help to prepare youth for physical changes.

Even if the adolescent is given the facts about what

is coming, it is never like actually experiencing it. The adolescent male is given a new voice that at first is unreliable, even embarrassing. Big feet make him clumsy. Muscles which can do more harm than he realizes, and sexual organs which he cannot fully understand. Girls are given hips and breasts that are perplexing and divulging, menstrual periods and mood swings that can be unwelcome and inconvenient. Adolescents may need to be reminded by parents that their bodies are sacred and that they will need to be good stewards of their health.

Process of Becoming

These changes make the separation from parents inevitable. The break in the dependency is as predetermined as the physical changes. Children need to grow up and leave home. The intuitive drive to separate from the very people who gave life and nurture is a powerful influence.

Adolescence is a process of becoming. It is intensely personal. Parents may be supportive, peers may give comfort, but in the end leaving childhood and becoming an adult is a singular journey. One about which adolescents have considerable ambivalence. This crossroads is a classic battle between emergence and terror. Emergence usually wins out but not without a price. A price paid in grief over the loss of innocence and of the parental relationship which will never again be the same. There are sizable fears of what is to come. Some adolescents even grieve the physical changes. It is as if they are being betrayed by their own bodies.

Adolescence is about being adult in body but a child in judgment. It is a dilemma that will take a decade to figure out. Most of the adult impulses and the adult capacities are present early in adolescence. Adolescents are physically strong. They are becoming attractive. Sexual intercourse and reproduction are possible. With the help of the school, they are learning factual knowledge that brings them into the adult world. In most respects they are adults.

The missing component is that their judgment has not yet fully matured. They have not had the life experiences that are needed to help them become effective critical thinkers. Their brain hormones are still in transition. The ability to do critical thinking assumes a platform of maturity and stability that they do not have yet.

It is hard for adolescents to understand adult concerns about safety, risk, and long-term consequences. Teens believe they are impervious to danger. Immune to death. Wisdom cannot be taught. It has to be learned. This creates tension between parents who want to protect and adolescents who want to experience life. It can seem like a never-ending battle. Gradually teens learn to exercise good judgment and parents accept the increase in autonomy.

Adolescence is also about transferring dependency from parents to peers. Peers are what psychologist Ron Taffel calls "the second family." So while adolescents appear to be gaining independence as they pull away from their parents, they are replacing one source of dependency with another. When teens reach this crossroad, someone has to meet their needs. While coaches, teachers, and youth advisors can help, it is ultimately the peers who offer support.

This is what makes it so frightening to parents. They know that the peers are not any wiser than their children. Sometimes less so. It is the blind leading the blind on very important life decisions. Few young adolescents want to be alone in their new world, and they give their loyalty over to the new "family." Their choices of music, clothing, movies, morality, and many other things are shaped by peers.

How Adolescents Act, Think, and Feel

It is primarily what adolescents do that gets the attention of parents. A lot of their behavior is very visible like the clothing and hairstyles they wear. They get our attention with their strongly expressed opinions or in the volume of the music in their cars. Their energy cannot be denied. They are always in motion, going to unknown places with undetermined purposes. In the process of creating a persona, adolescents do things that give them visibility and uniqueness in the outside world. It is almost as if they would be forgotten if they did not stand out. Being overlooked by peers is worse than being in conflict with parents and authority people.

Parents often find it hard to understand the excesses of their teens. There is no logic to wearing black lipstick or to music which hurts the ears. Parents get especially concerned about the choices that are dangerous or life altering. Their drinking and use of illegal drugs. More teens are smoking cigarettes. Many are sexually active. Their poor driving records are documented. Some are even physically violent.

For most adolescents, their flight from parents is less dramatic. It is more commonly seen in their frequent disagreements with parents. The hour of their curfew, who they date and how often. The kind of music they listen to. The condition of their bedrooms. How many nights they are allowed to be out. Even though their behavior may be less risky than that of some other adolescents, they still can present a challenge to parents.

Influences on Behavior

Adolescent behavior is influenced by many factors including the following:

1. The insecurity that comes from living in a body that is constantly changing. Often the body does not look quite right and does not work the way it should. Many adolescents do not like their noses, their hair, or their bodies. Their facial skin is often marred by acne. They are afraid they look weird. For some of them, the insecurity feeds the obsession that leads to anorexia or compulsive weight lifting. Many adolescents are relentlessly self-conscious. Sometimes this insecurity leads them to act out aggressively almost as a way of diverting attention away from the source of their anxiety.

2. The brain biochemistry tends to lead many adolescents into mood swings. The swings may not be frequent or intense, but they are difficult for parents to understand. Parents tend to scold or interrogate their teen when they have moods. Usually it does not help. Some teens may be depressed, and others can go through periods of obsessive-compulsiveness. These teens may need help through counseling and medication. Suicide is the third leading cause of teen death (Narramore and Lewis, *Parenting Teens,* p. 285). Moods need to be taken seriously by parents.

3. Teens are very affected by each other. They want to be accepted and will do almost anything to fit in. They tend to believe in the values of the peer culture even if those values put them in conflict with their parents or their own values.

4. Teens are victims of activity overload. They do too much and are fatigued. They often do not get enough

sleep. Their frenzied lives lead them into behavior that carries risk, but they cannot recognize it because their brains are flooded with too much activity. Their schoolwork, extracurriculars, part-time jobs, and other activities are sometimes more than they can handle.

5. Many parents set poor examples with their own lifestyles. They watch movies that feature violence and sexual promiscuity and give messages to their adolescents that there are not boundaries. They may need alcohol to feel comfortable at parties or smoke to "calm their nerves." Parents are a part of a society that gives an invitation to adolescents to experiment, to seek pleasure, and to have everything they want. Adolescents know that their behavior is similar to what they see in many of their role models.

6. Sometimes their behavior is a result of chaos in their homes. They may be reacting to absent or inconsistent structure or as an extension of conflict between the parents. Teens often feel caught in the middle when parents separate or divorce. Teens feel powerless to solve their parents' problems. Either in helping them bring order to their lives or in fixing marital problems.

7. The behavior of teens reflects the moral vacuum within. They are moving away from the guidance of the parents and have not yet developed belief systems of their own. What is in their conscience is fragile and often quite unsophisticated. They lack both the maturity and the moral courage to direct their behavior.

Parents' Role

When most couples chose to have children, they were not thinking at that moment of adolescents. They were instead thinking about a warm and cuddly child or an older child with whom they could toss baseball in the back yard. Adolescents are not interested much in doing either. They run from hugs, and they look up and down the street to make sure none of their friends will see them tossing a baseball with Dad.

Parenting adolescents is like trying to do a job for someone who does not want it done. Sort of like it must feel to collect taxes or to be a dentist who has to do a root canal. It's an important job. Somebody's got to do it. But the client is not really thrilled with what you are proposing. It has plenty of rewards, but the recipient of the service would be the last person to let you know. For some parents it is like they find themselves riding along on a roller coaster that they did not ask to get on. They discover that they cannot get off until the ride is over.

However, parenting adolescents can be rewarding. Many teens are reluctant to acknowledge it, but they still feel connected to their parents. Parents and adolescents have a whole lot of history together and, unless the adolescent is adopted, share similar genes. Even though hormones, peers, and some nasty culture wars may separate the two sides, the bond is still there. In spite of all the changes for adolescents, they remain the same people inside that they were when they were younger.

Parents try to believe the comforting stories of other people who have gone through the experiences. If those people survived maybe they can too. It is rewarding for them to see their children master skills in various areas and assume more responsibilities at school and home. Parents feel reassured when their youth go on service projects or write articles for the school newspapers.

Some parents and adolescents have trouble resolving the alienation that can come during this period.

They may choose to go their separate ways for many years. Adolescence can be a difficult time during which parents and teens make big mistakes in their relationships. Most find ways to repair the damage. If either side is unwilling to work on reconciliation, both lose. The unwillingness to resolve these conflicts often lead to additional relationship problems with other people. For teens it can mean conflictual relationships in dating. Poor decisions that may even effect their own marriages and eventually their own children.

Much of the success of parenting adolescents depends on the quality of the parenting in earlier stages. If there were effective boundaries, good preventive and corrective discipline, and a strong bond with the child, this stage will be more manageable. Although the emerging adolescents may seem like strangers, they really are not. All the good parenting done earlier will pay off. There may be some tests of the relationship, but the basic foundation has already been built that will reduce many of the risks.

Parenting during this stage will continue to require that parents manage their own lives and the family environment. Schedules are controlled. The margins for free time are protected. Careers are not allowed to steal from family time. Hobbies, recreation, travel away from the children will be contained. Lifestyle choices will be made which place God at the center of family life.

Materialism and the use of money to influence people are controlled. It is during this period that teens are earning money and developing attitudes about it. A family ethos of service will remain important. Telephone calls during meals, excessive use of television and computers, and other intrusions into family life will be avoided. Adolescence is in part about being out of control. If parents also fail to manage their lives, everyone edges toward chaos. Chaos is never good for anyone. It is even worse for adolescents.

Parents and Their Own Adolescence

When children become adolescents, some parents try to be close friends with them because the teen suddenly seems like an adult. Occasionally parents will begin to dress like their teens, listen to the same music, go to some of their concerts, and may even begin to act like them. Others may use the teens as confidants or as substitutes for companionship that is not coming from spouses or friends. When parents regress to the level of teens, they lose authority and respect. They also create problems for the teen who should be getting their friendship needs met from peers. Parent and teen roles that become blurred are harmful to both.

It is important for parents to have left their own adolescence behind by the time their first child reaches this stage. If parents are still rebelling or are resisting limits, they will not be able to set boundaries for their teens. In fact, the teens will most likely be encouraged to do high-risk behavior by the parents' attitudes. Some parents try to set standards for their teens that are different from the ones they live by. Teens see through the hypocrisy and ignore the parents. Parents who are unwilling to restrict themselves lose moral and behavioral authority.

A belief that is common among some parents is that teens need to do high-risk behaviors to get them "out of their system." Some call it "sowing their wild oats" and believe it was helpful to them when they were growing up. They may even take some pride in the fact that they still stretch the limits. While adolescence is in part about exploring new territory and experimenting with new feelings, there is no evidence that living dangerously is necessary or even helpful. When teens die in car accidents, nothing is gained. When they initiate pregnancies, they create lifelong consequences. Some who start smoking during this period will not stop until lung cancer or heart disease intervenes. Parents who live by this myth may become witnesses to teens who do not.

Starting Early

It is important for parents to express clearly their expectations to teens early in this period. It is much harder to make boundaries after teens are into patterns that make parents uncomfortable. Teens need to know curfew times, dating frequency, limits on their jobs, how their money is to be used, and similar standards from the outset.

Teens can give their opinions about the standards, and sometimes parents can compromise. The process of working out the standards together can help teens develop good problem-solving abilities and feel a useful sense of power. It is important for parents to have good listening skills and to be good at negotiating. While parents are expected to have the final authority, they can exercise their authority lovingly. Giving teens freedom without boundaries is not a gift. If the boundaries are clear from the beginning, teens will find this stage to be truly freeing.

Gray Areas

What makes parenting teens so difficult is that a lot of their behavior is in the gray zone. What music is bad and how bad is it? Should they be allowed to go to this rock concert and not to that one? Should a sixteen-year-old own a car? Is it acceptable to stay overnight at a boyfriend's house if the parents are there? Adolescents invent ambiguity. The more gray the better. They make their parents squirm. They are not trying to make parents miserable. They raise questions because they are learning to think for themselves in situations that are complex. If everything were clearly right or wrong, teens would not develop the skills that they will need later when life is even more ambiguous.

Parents who are skillful at handling gray areas are the ones who know when to say "no" to requests that are clearly outside the boundaries, and "oh" to requests that might be uncomfortable but low in risk. A caring parent would say "no" to a request to stay overnight at the boyfriend's house when the parents are not home but perhaps "oh" when a group of teens are staying overnight and the parents are home. Successful parents are firmly flexible.

Some of the ambiguity also comes on the matter of teen privacy. Teens like to consider their rooms as sacrosanct. They want them to be off-limits to parents. They also like to talk on the phone without being overheard. They do not want their mail opened by parents. Teens do not like the "twenty questions" routine from their parents about their activities. Their privacy is a part of developing a sense of selfhood. For the most part, parents need to respect the wishes of the teen, even if it causes some anxiety for them.

However, when a teen is clearly in trouble, the rules may change. If there are unmistakable signs of depression, using drugs or alcohol, spending large amounts of time on the computer, or if the teen is sexually active, parents can cross the privacy boundary. If teens leave notes or diaries on their dressers, it may be important to read them. Overhearing a phone call discussing high-risk behavior gives parents the right and obligation to be involved. At times teens need to be protected from themselves. When they give clues, parents need to be alert. Teens may even want parents to invade their privacy and rescue them.

Role of Mentors

Teens, especially those who live in single parent families, need other adults in their lives as auxiliary parents. Even the best parents are not enough to meet all of their needs. They need youth advisors, youth pastors, coaches, mentors, teachers, and even work supervisors to supplement what parents can do for them. In a sense it is a part of a natural progression away from home. In a few short years, teens will be totally on their own. They will then need to develop support systems that will guide and encourage them.

During these years, parents should actively help their teens to seek out these important people. Some teens are fortunate enough to be involved in churches where it happens automatically. When the mentoring happens spontaneously (i.e., as with a teacher) parents need to know this person and be assured that the mentor shares the parents' most important values. A good mentor to teens can make parents more effective and can help teens through perhaps the most stressful periods in their lives.

Helping the Teen Plan for the Future

Teens face increasing pressure about their life choices. Early in the high school years, they are required to decide whether to prepare for college or for a trade. While that choice may be difficult, for those who want to attend college the process becomes more complicated. By their junior year college-bound students are inundated with invitations from institutions that are competing for their enrollment. Students with good grades, high test scores, or who are gifted in athletics or performance arts are recruited with special intensity.

It is important for parents to assist teens with these decisions. Can fifteen-year-olds decide whether they want to enter a profession or a trade without guidance from parents? They are just beginning to figure what it means to be an adolescent and to find their way around the high school.

For those who choose college, how many are prepared for the pressures of the college recruiters when they are seventeen? Many are influenced by the amount of scholarship aid they get or the potential for playing a sport at a big-name school. For some the choice is based on the reputation of a particular department at a school or on the prestige of a school. Others are influenced by the slickness of the publicity, the personality of the recruiter, how nice the campus looks, or even how close to home the school is located.

Unfortunately parents are sometimes influenced by the same things the students are. They can lose their objectivity in helping the students make the best choices. To them, too, the less money they need to pay the better. And they can get caught up in the excitement of having their child gain notoriety through playing a sport or through going to a prestigious school. Some parents want their child to attend a college that is close to home.

Important factors can be overlooked when making decisions about college. People often fail to recognize that most schools meet the stiff standards of the accrediting agencies for their region and that students get a good education almost anywhere. They also fail to look at the fact that many students go to graduate school at large universities with well-known departments.

The most significant factor for parents and students is whether the school will be compatible with the spiritual and social values of the family and of the support community. If it is not, students will be pressured into accepting the standards of the new community. Friends and potential spouses will be drawn from this base.

How will they influence the future choices of the young adults? Will they continue to connect with the values that have been important? The college years are extremely significant in shaping the direction for adulthood. Parents can play an active part in the choice.

For those teens who do not continue their schooling, parents can encourage them to do a term of voluntary service with a national or area church agency or perform a service in their local communities. Some can do short-term service through agencies that assist communities after natural disasters.

Congregations need to find ways to appeal to the post-high school youths who are living in the community and give them meaningful assignments in the church. It is helpful for teens to begin to expand their worldview. Parents and the church community can provide them with a larger vision and with some structure that can help them make good choices for their lives.

Freedom Fences

1. We acknowledge the right that our teens have to develop independence, and we will not hold onto the teens for our own needs.

2. We will continue to be full-time parents to our teens, even though we may at times seem to be unwelcome. That means controlling our jobs and other outside interests.

3. We will continue to put structure and order in our lives and in our homes. That will mean making the kind of choices for ourselves that are consistent with what we want for our teens.

4. We will welcome our teens' friends into our

home and will learn to know the friends' parents.

5. We will take an active part in creating alliances of parents of teens to discuss common standards and to advocate for responsible teen behavior.

6. We will be comfortable setting fair standards before they are needed for our teens and will have the courage to enforce them. That includes not accepting the belief that our teen needs to engage in high-risk behavior.

7. We will be tolerant of low-risk behavior that may annoy us but may be important to the teen.

8. We will stay active in parenting our post-high school young adults until successful transitions to adulthood are made.

Questions

1. Why is it necessary for teens to experience some separation from their parents?
2. If part of growing up is learning, why is it not better for teens to learn things for themselves?
3. Because standards change from one generation to the next, how can I be sure that my standards still are valid?
4. What do I do if my teen refuses to do what I say?
5. What kinds of consequences are effective when my teen jumps over the fences?
6. If all the other parents allow their teens to do things I object to, what can I do to get my teen to

listen to me?
7. How can parents work with other parents to set up community structures?
8. What can I do to help my teen choose faith and baptism?
9. How can I influence my teen to choose a church college? How important is that to you?

Activity

Make a list of the decisions that are "no" and those that are "oh." How did you make your decisions? Do you ever change your mind and reverse your decisions?

Bibliography

Beekman, Susan, and Jeanne Holmes
1993 *Battles, Hassles, Tantrums and Tears: Strategies for Coping with Conflict and Making Peace at Home.* New York: Hearst Books.

Bingham, Mindy, and Sandy Stryker
1995 *Things Will Be Different for My Daughter*. New York: Penguin Books.

Elkind, David
1994 *Ties That Stress: The New Family Imbalance.* Cambridge: Harvard University Press.
1984 *All Grown Up and No Place to Go: Teenagers in Crisis*. Reading: Addison Wesley Publishing Co.

Hersch, Patricia
1998 *A Tribe Apart*. New York: Fawcett Co.

Narramore, Bruce, and Vern Lewis
1990 *Parenting Teens*. Wheaton: Tyndale House Publisher.

Pipher, Mary
1994 *Reviving Ophelia*. New York: Ballantine Books.

Sandmaeir, Marian
1996 "More Than Love" in *The Family Therapy Networker*. May/June, p. 20.
Taffel, Ron
1996 "The Second Family" in *The Family Therapy Networker.* May/June, p. 36.

12

The Joys and the Challenges of the Middle Agers

And whoever does not provide for relatives, and especially for family members, has denied the faith and is worse than an unbeliever. 1 Timothy 5:8 (NRSV)

Children should not have to save up for parents, but parents for children. 2 Corinthians 12:14 (NIV)

Caught in the Middle

At no other period in life than middle age will most people have so many family members depending on them. Could Paul have been aware of how important the assignment would become to twenty-first-century Christians? He was speaking at a time when the life span was about one half of what it is today. Would he still say the same thing? If he had attended a workshop on the "sandwich generation," would it have changed his opinion? Providing for relatives may vary from one person to the next, but people in their middle years often have plenty of family members to look after.

This comes at a time when careers are at their peak

levels of responsibility. When the pressures of family responsibilities are supposed to diminish. The nest is empty, and the heaviest debt is past. Now there are nice quiet evenings alone to read. The stereo and the TV have been reclaimed. Dinner is quiet and leisurely. French fries, coke, and pizza are no longer staples. The glossy brochures for cruises or trips across the country now suddenly seem appealing. This is what the middle agers were waiting for. What all of those sacrifices were for.

But, alas, an adult child asks to come back home. He or she ran into tough luck on a job or a roommate got married. A child is coming back home temporarily after a marriage ran into trouble. Maybe the young adult is in a marriage that is going very well . . . three children well. These young parents want to continue their careers and want you to help them with childcare.

If full-time grandparenting is too much, how about part-time? Even ten hours a week would help a lot. If not that, maybe every Friday night so they can have a night off from their children? Then there are Grandparents Days at nursery school, Little League games, and ballet class recitals. Not to mention birthdays. Middle agers are faced with tough dilemmas. Many are blessed with wonderful grandchildren, but wonderful enough to give up a round of golf to see a grandson play the part of a pumpkin in the Thanksgiving play? Did anyone say it was going to be easy? Where is Paul when we need him?

While all of these existential crises are presenting themselves, the phone rings with Mom on the other end saying that Dad is showing signs of forgetfulness. He lost his keys for the third time this week. The neighbor boy is on vacation and cannot mow the yard, and there is a question about a medical form that must be filled out before the next doctor's appointment. "Would it be possible for you to come over tonight? It's all right if you can't, but I'm afraid Dad could wander off." The middle agers agonize over balancing their responsibilities to their parents and their commitments to their spouses. Welcome to the middle years!

Dealing with Young Adult Children

When the adolescent child walks across the stage to receive a high school diploma, something more than the graduation is happening. That adolescent is entering adulthood. Until this point parents played a major role in nurturing, protecting, and disciplining their teen. Up to now the teen made few totally independent decisions. After graduation, the role of the parents changes dramatically. Their adolescent child has become a young adult who is capable of going away to college or of maintaining full-time work. The previous role of the parents has ended.

From this point on, young adults are expected to be self-directed. Whether they survive in college or on their jobs is largely up to them. Parents can show interest and offer advice but cannot write the term papers for the college student or complete a difficult task for the working young adult. With this increase in independence comes a decline in parental authority. Parents and young adults will test out this new relationship in the months following graduation. It is an uncomfortable stage for both. Clashes occur frequently. As parents and young adults gradually separate emotionally, young adults establish new identities. Parents wonder where they fit in. What is their new role with their young adult?

Young Adulthood Has Changed

Parenting young adults is different than it was several generations ago because young adulthood has changed. More young adults are single. While in an earlier period, serious contact and dating began in the late teens with marriage happened in the early twenties, today these are delayed. The average man is twenty-seven years old and the woman is twenty-five when they marry. The meaning that has for young adults and for their parents is immense.

In the past, parents could stay involved in the young adult's life because their dating tended to bring them into more contact with each other. In a sense they had more in common. Coupling was something they could both understand. When the young adults married and had children, bonds developed around shared experiences. Now with young adults single into their mid-twenties and into a lifestyle that most parents did not experience, they are in different worlds. And for a much longer time.

Not that young adults in times past were innately more mature. It was their marital status and their role as parents that initiated changes in their lifestyles. It meant that at least one of the spouses had to have a job that could meet the expenses. Income was a necessity. Reality had a way of limiting personal indulgences. Traveling impromptu through the country or doing step aerobics at the health club were often not options. Young adults were less concerned with a weekly round of golf than with the weekly trip to the grocery store. Adulthood started earlier. Parents were more comfortable around their young adults because their lifestyles were similar.

Young Adult and Sexual Choices

Young adults approach their sexuality differently than their parents did. What is different today is that many young adults are more active sexually because of delayed marriage. Sexual passions have not changed, but attitudes about sexual expression have. It is common for young adults to have had several sexual partners before they marry. Many have lived with partners in simulated marriage without long-term commitments. Because of profound cultural changes in attitudes about sexual morality, some single young adults have little motivation to postpone sex until marriage.

In spite of evidence that open sexual expression carries significant emotional and medical risks, many young adults are unconvinced. Either they do not believe the studies or they are unconcerned that the results will be as bad as described. Critical thinking is placed on hold by young adults who believe that the previous standard for sexual behavior is outdated and moralistic.

Parents are unsure of their role. Either they approve of their young adults' choices or they risk losing the relationships. Many give tacit approval. Some who do not give approval experience years of tension. Some parents have become numbed by the promiscuity or by a succession of potential in-laws to whom they attach and unattach.

When the young adult lives in a common-law relationship, parents are denied the comfort of relating to the partner as a genuine family member. The tentativeness can impact the connection between the parents and the potential in-law. If the couple marries, the celebration can be deprived of some of the specialness. The sacrament has been diminished.

Sometimes young adults blame parents for their choices, believing they were either too strict or too lenient. Indeed, no parents handle their roles perfectly. It can be helpful for parents to apologize for their mistakes and to be open about their personal failures.

Moments of openness between parents and adult children can lead to a new level of authenticity in the relationship. These times can provide teachable moments for the parents to discuss how uncommitted relationships with companions can be unfulfilling, how important it is to choose the right spouse, and the reasons for sexual boundaries. The role of a parent does not stop when the young adult graduates from high school. It just changes.

However, it is important for young adults to accept responsibility for their choices, especially choices that have painful endings. To acknowledge their part in failed relationships, unwanted pregnancies, venereal disease, and sexual excesses. As adults they will live with the consequences of their behavior; to blame their parents for being either too strict or too lenient misses the point.

Young Adults in a Material World

Young adults have access to more money and more possessions than ever. Their purchasing power is not lost on the credit card companies or on the suppliers in the marketplace. Clothing, electronic items, high-tech connections, cell phones and sports utility vehicles offer the good life. Most young adults participate in the material world but are not consumed by it. They make wise investments and live within their means. They may like nice things, but they do not depend on them to make them happy. Many actively reject the symbols of affluence and the pretentiousness of some people who are wealthy. They are redefining simple living for their generation.

Unfortunately, some young adults start adulthood with credit problems that will follow them for years. Some have parents who will rescue them. Some will escape through bankruptcy. Others will get themselves out of trouble through working overtime or through a second job. All who spend beyond their means have to live with the results. "An adult who does not stand on his own financially is still a child. To be adult you must live within your means and pay for your failures" (Townsend and Cloud, *Boundaries,* p. 126).

Parents may have contributed to the problems through their own spending patterns. The young adults may now repeat the same lifestyle. This may be an opportunity for both to change their patterns. Middle agers need to model restraint and offer advice about budgeting. Parents indeed have a role. Coaching the adult child on restraint before spending is out of control is better than subsidizing a lifestyle of excess spending. The best gift parents can give to young adults is an understanding of restraint and sacrifice. And maybe to teach some lessons in reality.

Young Adults and Spirituality

Some young adults continue on the spiritual path of their childhood. They may attend the same church with their parents and grandparents. Some may even sit in the family pew. As young adults they may be active in teaching Sunday school, singing in the choir, or coordinating summer Bible school.

However, often this is a period when young adults appear to abandon the faith of their childhood. Some lean towards religious skepticism and may not connect with any church. Others may go the opposite direction and become involved in new types of religious expressions. It is hard for parents to be neutral about the choices on either end. Young adults may not be comfortable with the church of their childhood, especially after college. It can seem out of date and old-fashioned. They may be offended because members treat them as if they were still the eighteen-year-olds who left the community earlier.

It is helpful for parents to support young adults as they explore new expressions of their religious faith. Perhaps encouraging involvement in congregations that have large young adult groups. Perhaps through helping to create new young adult small group assemblies. Gatherings that meet Saturday nights instead of Sunday morning often appeal to young adults. Creative programming is often important to those who are searching for something new.

Because of their high energy levels and their idealism, many are drawn to unconventional churches. Some young adults find meaningful faith expression through terms of service abroad or in peace and justice projects. Others discover a new level of spirituality through charismatic worship with bands and worship teams. Young adults are seldom traditional and often puzzle their parents. However, parents can never stop caring about young adults' spiritual choices. These choices will be important through the rest of their lives.

Young Adults Living at Home

Today more young adults are living at home. While some may never have left, others return after college or because living arrangements elsewhere did not work out. Whatever the circumstances, it may not be easy for the parents or for the young adults. Both sides can have trouble knowing what their new relationship should be. The parental authority is changing, and the choices being made by young adults may not always sit well with their parents. In a sense, both sides are uncomfortable partners in a situation which neither particularly has chosen.

Most parents are ready to have young adults move

into independence. They would welcome an empty nest. But they are reluctant to ask young adults to move out for fear of offending them. Maybe the young adults cannot afford to move out. Most would prefer to be on their own, even though some have not yet shed the last remnants of their dependency. Home is comfortable. It is nice to have so many things being done for them and, for many, the price is hard to beat.

A very small segment of young adults who do not leave home cannot do so because of some kind of emotional impairment. Illnesses like schizophrenia, manic-depression, depression, and similar conditions come to the surface at this age. Whether the conditions are totally biochemical in origin or from an inability to accept the pressures of adult responsibility is not always clear. It may be a combination of factors.

When young adults become ill, parents need to find treatment for them through mental health professionals. Usually medication is useful. When the condition is more severe, it may be necessary for the young adult to live in a protected setting. It is very important for parents to become a part of support groups, like No Longer Alone in our community, which help parents receive comfort and insight from each other. Often these groups help convey to parents that they are not responsible for their young adult's condition.

Living at home as a young adult is a privilege. The home belongs to the parents. Young adults may be welcome guests, but they stay with the permission of the hosts. That means that some basic household guidelines still apply. Young adults need to inform the parents when they will be home for meals or when they will be in at night. They have responsibilities and participate in the house chores. Unless there are some unusual circumstances, young adults pay for room and board.

Staying at home gratis does nothing to prepare them for being on their own. Instead it creates "the perpetual child syndrome." "When parents continue providing services for adult children, they keep the child from emotionally leaving home" (Townsend and Cloud, *Boundaries,* p. 126). Living at home can be a temporary arrangement for an adult child. It should be a time for continued growth on the path to self-reliance and not another way of postponing adulthood.

Middle Agers as Grandparents

As with any role, grandparenting is something most middle agers have to learn. Having been a parent helps. Babies still look the same, cry for the same reasons, and respond to the old tricks that worked for generations. Disposable diapers make life simpler for the parents, and the equipment for children is better. New grandparents are comforted when they realize that the job has not changed that much. Even though middle agers have not cared for young children for several decades, many have not lost the knack.

However, grandparenting is different than parenting. The children belong to someone else, have different routines, and some new genes that make life more interesting. Grandparents are older and get tired sooner than when they had young children. The challenge for new grandparents is to know where they fit in.

Because people are living longer, more middle agers can expect to play an active role as grandparents. Just a few generations ago, most grandchildren did not know all of their grandparents because people then did not live as long. Now grandparents have an opportunity to play important parts in grandchildren's lives. Marlene only knew one grandparent. He was a good-natured man who came to live with the family some years after he became widowed. He was an important part of the family and had an honored seat at the dinner table. He was not as involved with the grandchildren in the ways many grandparents are today. As today's middle agers become grandparents, they are generally healthier and younger in mind and body. Grandparents go kayaking, camping, hiking, and shoot baskets in the driveway. Grandmothers may even take ballet lessons with their granddaughters. They may even ride the roller coaster together at the amusement park.

The role of grandparenting is changing because society is different. It is less formal. Jerry hardly feels like a patriarch when he is crawling on the floor with the grandchildren. Marlene hardly resembles a matriarch after the grandchildren have had a face painting session with her. Maybe parents and grandparents are both more relaxed these days. While it is important for grandchildren to respect their elders, it is probably good that some of the arbitrary barriers are removed. Grandparents need to be approachable and authentic. Grandparents become a nice alternative when grandchildren and their parents need a break from each other.

Grandparents as Childcare Workers

Grandparents are becoming a resource for childcare as more mothers are pursuing careers outside the home. This plan, in some ways, is clearly positive for the parents and the grandchildren because grandparents have a personal interest in the well-being of the grandchild. Parents can relax knowing that their child is safe and loved. However, serving as a parent substitute will change the relationship between grandparent and grandchild. A parental bond will form. The child will have two sets of parents. The grandparent will become both a disciplinarian and a caregiver. Perhaps the greatest loss comes when the grandparents become too familiar. Grandmothers and grandfathers who remain in their traditional roles are part magical because of their distance, their uncommoness, and their specialness.

Helpful Grandparenting

To be most helpful, grandparents need to maintain a secondary role to the parents. They are supportive and not primary. They are available in times of crises, like when one of the parents is sick or involved in responsibilities that require their time. Increasingly, grandparents are called on when parents experience marital problems, especially when those problems lead to divorce. They may also be asked to be involved when a grandchild is born outside of marriage. Grandparents can be the primary security for grandchildren for a period of time. Grandparents only serve as a backup to parents and relinquish their positions when the parents resume their roles.

Grandparents can be helpful when they volunteer to give parents a night off or even a weekend away for their wedding anniversary. This gives parents a time to recover from the daily demands and return to parenting with new energy. In some cultures, grandmothers play an important role in teaching mothers parenting skills.

While there is some potential that this role can be overextended, the oral parenting tradition can be invaluable. Sharing wisdom about effective feeding patterns, how to get children to sleep through the night, or how to deal with temper tantrums are experiences the grandparents have gone through before. This wisdom can be shared in a way that can be helpful. Grandparents and parents both need to update their childrearing knowledge and skills.

Grandparents can give to grandchildren the comfort

of knowing that extended family exists beyond the immediate family. It is comforting for them to know that there is a broad foundation of support and that extended family gives identity. They are there for celebration. It is for a sense of belonging, especially in a world that is losing a sense of community and that has the rootlessness of suburbia.

Grandparents offer the wonderful gift of mystery to grandchildren. A special way of fishing. Of storytelling. Of baking pies. When grandpa finds a frog, it should be like no other frog on earth. When grandma puts a Band-Aid on a scratch, it should have special healing powers. While parents are encumbered with commonness, grandparents are given a role of transcendence.

Grandparents who live at some distance and may only see their grandchildren infrequently can still have a close relationship with them. They can keep in touch by telephone, cards or letters, and e-mail. Those contacts are special. Relationships can be built during the extended visits. There is a something special about having grandparents stay overnight. That is something that grandparents who live close by rarely do.

Because grandparents come in all different ages and are younger for their first grandchildren than they are for their last, the role will vary. Obviously a forty-five-year-old grandparent is able to do some physical activities that a seventy-year-old cannot do. Although seventy-year-olds are getting younger these days, not too many of them sleep overnight in the tree house with the grandchildren. Or go down the slide with them at the playground. The older grandparents are the more they have to depend on their creativity. The best stories come from people who have gray hair and whose voices have just a bit of a quaver. Whose lines in the face suggest to grandchildren a special kind of wisdom. Grandparents are important at any age.

Unhelpful Grandparenting

Grandparents can be hurtful when they are too involved in the life of a family. The parents and their children have a right to privacy. The integrity of that unit needs to be respected. Visits or calls that are too frequent become intrusive. They place the grandparents in a more primary role that is appropriate. Intrusiveness prevents parents and their children from bonding and from developing problem-solving skills.

When families function as primary units, they can be creative in finding ways to grow and explore. Their free time should be spent in discovering new mountains, canoeing, even playing in the backyard. These are, for the most part, events for the immediate family unit. Grandparents can participate from time to time, but the free time belongs to the parents and their children. The Genesis passage that suggests that men and women should leave their parents to cleave to each other did not mean only until children were born! Grandparents have a special role but it needs fences.

Grandparents are unhelpful when they undermine the authority of parents. They are asked to support the discipline, routine, and the standards of the parents. An unhelpful grandparent gives candy to a two-year-old an hour before dinner. A helpful grandparent tucks a stick of sugarless gum away to give to the grandchild at the end of a church service. An unhelpful grandparent lets young children play until they drop from exhaustion. A helpful grandparent spends time quietly reading and singing to children to help them fall asleep at naptime. Grandparents can lavish their grandchildren with love by using common sense and having respect for the developmental needs of the grandchildren.

Only in unusual situations, when grandparents believe the parents are being abusive or neglectful, should they intervene and then only in private to the parent. It is important that grandparents not allow themselves to become allied with a grandchild against a parent. If that happens the parent needs to insist on changes.

Grandparenting is not about making up through a grandchild what they did not give that grandchild's parent. Sometimes grandparents try to do that through giving love, time, and affection to the grandchildren. Sometimes it is done through material things. The missed opportunities of the past will not be made right through a grandchild. It usually makes the hurt deeper for the parent who missed out as a child. It tends to indulge a grandchild in ways that are damaging.

Grandparents do not step into the parenting role because they believe the grandchildren are not being taken care of properly. While they may be correct in their observations, if they enter a family as rescuers, they undermine the integrity of the family unit. It is much better to offer financial help for parenting classes, recommend good reading material, or encourage counseling instead of trying to take over the parenting. Grandparents can model love, patience, and kindness. Grandparents can be teachers when they share remembrances of their difficult moments in parenting. Grandparents can be a wonderful source of encouragement to the parents without fixing the problem.

Some middle agers do not want to be involved in grandparenting at all. They are too busy with their own activities. Some are concerned that grandchildren could damage and soil their house. Others say that they raised their family, and they do not want to do it again. But the middle ager's children need them to be involved. The grandchildren are left with something very important missing from their life if they are detached. Most of all, the grandparents lose a special opportunity to be involved in a very rewarding time of their life.

Middle Agers and Aging Parents

These days many middle agers have elderly parents. The number of elderly people in the Western world continues to increase. In fact, the fastest growing age group (by percent) is the group over 100 years old. While middle agers may still have a young adult living at home and may be offering supportive care to grandchildren, they may also be making daily trips down the road to attend to their ailing parents. Talk about overload! Many middle agers find that caring for their parents is the most taxing of all. Perhaps it is because they know it is a commitment that can only lead to increased responsibility. The aging process is not a welcome one for the middle ager or for the parent.

The Relationship Extends from Earlier Times

Sometimes the relationships between the middle agers and their parents are complicated by unresolved conflicts that began many years earlier. Maybe they clashed frequently, were too interdependent, or were never close. During childhood they felt responsible for making their parents happy. When parents begin their decline, the previous problems in the relationship become magnified. What complicates things now is that the parent and the child have to reverse roles. The parent who once cared for the child is now being cared for by the child.

Several years ago, Marlene's elderly father had problems with bladder control. Her mother convinced him to wear adult diapers, but he resisted changing the diapers. Obviously he felt humiliated. He had a noticeable odor, and Marlene's mother asked her to help convince him to change the diapers more often. In a firm but kind way, Marlene talked with him about the problem. He listened with discomfort and maybe a little resentment, but he agreed to be more attentive to his personal care. The reversal of roles was not easy for either of them.

As senior parents decline in health, they often suffer from a loss of self-esteem, power, and purpose. They have to give up so many things that are important to them. Most have to turn over the keys to their cars. Many are physically less mobile. Some have to curtail cooking because they forget to turn off the stove. Many give up their houses when they are unable to maintain them. They lose their freedom.

With these losses, middle agers have to increase their involvement. They become the sources of transportation. They have the responsibility for mowing the yards and doing other maintenance. They coordinate doctor's appointments, balance checkbooks, and do many other tasks. Often it is the middle agers who live closest to the parents who bears the heaviest burden.

With many more adult siblings living in communities distant from elderly parents, it is important that creative solutions be found to balance out the responsibilities. Certainly they can offer their homes for either long-term or short-term care. While many elderly parents enjoy visiting their middle-aged children, most will not uproot their lives for longer periods. They want to visit with their friends and continue attending church and community activities.

Some middle agers may spend some of their vacation time with their elderly parents to relieve the siblings who have primary care. All should offer financial help to secure medical and social services that lift the burdens from the local siblings. The expenses of the local siblings should always be reimbursed by the distant siblings if the parent does not do so. All siblings should take an active part in thinking about and planning for their elderly parents. These burdens should never fall on the shoulders of the siblings who are at home.

Sometimes it is possible to share some of the responsibility by hiring caretakers, cleaning persons, Meals on Wheels, and or engaging a visiting nurse agency. But often the needs eventually exceed these services, and the parent requires nursing home care. The decision is always hard for the parent and the family. Not only can it feel like rejection to the parent but it also means a further loss of independence and an acknowledgment that life is coming to a close.

Some seniors feel comforted by the full-time care they receive in a nursing home and get a second wind. Their nutrition improves, and their medications are managed better. They make new friends and attend activities in the nursing home. At least for a time, some nursing home residents improve the quality of their lives. In spite of the initial improvement some seniors show in nursing homes, most people would rather be well and at home.

At the nursing home, the nice furniture, colorful walls, and cheery staff are all helpful, but they cannot remove the fact that the senior is in an institution. There is the realization that their health is declining. It is hard for many middle agers to deal with these facts. Some struggle with guilt for playing a part in placing parents in nursing homes.

End-of-life decisions are difficult to face. While modern medicine has undoubtedly extended life, it is a mixed blessing. It has allowed people to live longer and more meaningful lives. However, it has artificially maintained some seniors in a state that few of them would choose. The vaccines, nutritional supplements, and other forms of supportive care may be postponing the very death that would be welcomed by many seniors. If death is prevented for the moment, these measures do not provide a meaningful life. For many people the well-intentioned interventions sustain a body but trap a soul.

End-of-life questions often center on the so-called heroic life-saving measures. Many seniors have living wills that forbid their use. However, it is much harder to decide about how much of the standard care should be given. Should a person who has lived a long and meaningful life and is now incapacitated be vaccinated to prevent the flu or pneumonia? Should she or he get corrective surgery that may add another year of existence to a life that is empty?

Middle Agers Finding a Balance

Even too much of a good thing can be wrong. Middle agers need to have a life beyond their children, grandchildren, and parents. They may still have careers that are important to them as well as friendships that will continue to be vital to them in the years ahead. After all, grandchildren grow up just like children did. They are given for but a season and then they are gone.

Middle agers must have other interests and hobbies to energize them. Church and small groups are often central parts of the lives of middle agers. Many couples walk or play golf together. Vacations can be times of relaxation and growing closer. However, to devote a disproportionate amount of time to extended family creates an imbalance. It leaves a vacuum that will certainly be felt at a later time. It keeps the middle ager from experiencing the richness of a broader life during this period. Carving out time for relationships is vital.

There are many dilemmas that middle agers must face. Middle age is not a time that is as free as most would have imagined when they were in the midst of raising families and paying mortgages. It is a period filled with surprises. Many of them pleasant. Some of them perplexing. If middle agers take responsibility for managing their lives and those they care for, it can indeed be a rewarding period of time. Freedom within fences.

Freedom Fences

1. Treat adult children with respect, listening carefully to their ideas. Allow for some differences of opinions.

2. Be clear in establishing house rules when adult children live at home. The goal is to help them achieve full adulthood through being financially and emotionally independent, including caring for their own personal needs.

3. When adult children experience difficulties, assist them in getting the help they need. That is without protecting them or for paying for their mistakes.

4. Be available to offer nurture and care to grandchildren in a supportive role while respecting the integrity of the nuclear family.

5. Talk with elderly parents openly about their wishes for long-term care and end-of-life issues.

6. Keep a balance between family needs and the needs of elderly parents. Establish clear schedules with siblings or other caregivers.

7. Preserve time for you and your spouse to enjoy each other during these middle years. Nurture outside friendships and enrich your hobbies.

Questions

1. How long should a young adult live with parents? What are the alternatives?
2. Why is it important for young adults to be fully independent?
3. How can giving love and care to grandchildren be harmful?
4. How can I know when meeting my needs are more important than meeting those of my grandchildren's family?
5. How should I respond when my adult child is making choices that I cannot support?
6. How much time should be spent in giving care to adult children, grandchildren, and elderly parents?
7. Why is it so hard to say no when my elderly parent asks me for help? How can I know if the help is really needed?
8. How can I tell when I am being selfish and when I have given enough?

Activity

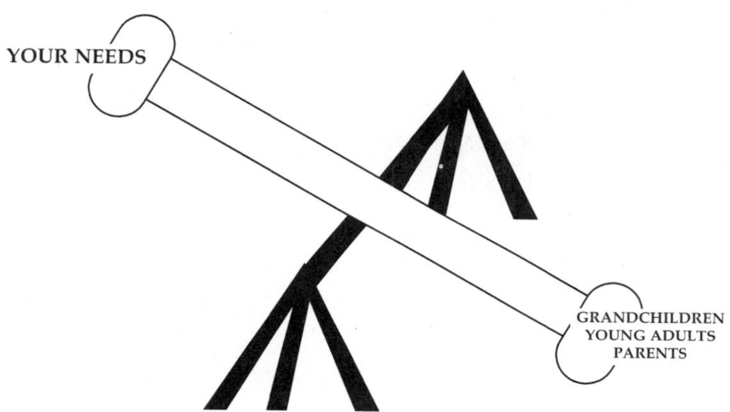

Put your needs on the one side and the needs of the other family members to whom you are giving care on the other side. Is it balanced? What can you do to balance your seesaw?

Bibliography

Evans, Debra
1997 *Ready or Not, You're a Grandparent*. New York: Chariot Victor Publishing.

Fowler, Ruth
1998 *As We Grow Old: How Adult Children and Their Parents Can Face Issues with Candor and Grace.* Valley Forge: Judson Press.

Molloy, William
1996 *Caring for Your Parents in Their Senior Years.* New York: Firefly Books.

Townsend, John, and Henry Cloud
1992 *Boundaries*. Grand Rapids: Zondervan Publishing.

Weibe, Katie Funk
1993 *Life After 50*. Newton: Faith & Life Press.

13

Freedom Stories

The stories that follow are courageous stories of ordinary people. They will not make the front pages of newspapers and will not win any awards for high drama. But they are the stuff upon which freedom is built. They illustrate the core of what contained living is all about. Freedom stories have always been told and hopefully always will be. In a sense they have no beginning or end. While some of the stories are identified by author others prefer to remain anonymous.

1. Celebrating Celibacy

"The Lord is my chosen portion and my cup; you hold my lot. The boundary lines have fallen for me in pleasant places; I have a goodly heritage." Psalm 16:5-6 (NRSV)

During my college years, I became acquainted with Reba Place Fellowship, an intentional Christian community springing from Anabaptist roots. As a young Christian confused and intimidated by the vocational, ethical, and lifestyle choices ahead of me as I was about to enter the adult work world, I was attracted to community. It presented me with a viable way to answer

Jesus' call to become his disciple in the context of a committed fellowship of believers also seeking to follow his way in swimming upstream against the many seductive and destructive cultural currents of our times. So at the early, vulnerable age of 21, I committed myself and my resources to the Lord and a fallible group of people covenanting to share money, property, decision making, common spiritual disciples, and life together.

I fully expected to meet a life partner, marry, have children, and replicate the life modeled for me by my Christian parents. But over the past 25 years at Reba Place, that has not been my path. During this time there have been disappointments, struggles, and wonderful opportunities that I have experienced as a long-term single woman committed to a celibate lifestyle. Though I live surrounded by brothers and sisters who offer me close, long-term relationships, I have my moments of loneliness, longing, and grief over the children I will never bear. Yet I have had the satisfaction of nurturing many spiritual children as a full-time pastor of a growing church I helped to plant. I have had opportunities for service, graduate education, and international travel I likely would not have had at this point in life had I been married with kids.

Sometimes I get fed up with my covenant partners in community. We have been going through many rocky stretches together. I find Paul's words in Philippians 4:11 about learning to find contentment with whatever his lot to be descriptive of the choice I have before me every day in my single, celibate state. G. K. Chesterton makes a similar point in saying, "True contentment is a real, even an active, virtue—not only affirmative but creative. It is the power of getting out of any situation all there is in it."

Instead of looking around at which pasture might be

greener and what I might be missing, I have resolved to commit all that I am and have to God and the people God has put me with, trusting that living within these boundary lines will yield the "goodly heritage" God has for me. I have discovered over and over that God is trustworthy in giving me my portion and filling my cup.—**Sally Schreiner**

2. Stay-at-Home Dad

Jeff: Our first son, Jake, was conceived while we were in voluntary service with a church relief and service agency. When our term of service ended, Faith was about three months pregnant, and we both needed to get jobs. It was always our assumption that one of us would stay home with our kids if it was possible financially. The only question was who that would be. At that point we felt it made sense for me to get a full-time job and for Faith to find part-time work.

Faith: I was looking forward to being Mom and didn't mind being the one to stay home. I'm a registered nurse and was able to find work at a retirement center. I worked twenty hours a week, so we only needed babysitting six times a month. I did have to work every other weekend, so Jeff got the chance to be with Jake then. This seemed to work well, and we continued this arrangement through the birth of our second child, Marcy, three years later.

Jeff: During this time, I worked in a print shop in a supervisory position that also involved a lot of production work. I enjoyed much of what I did, but I was required to put in a lot of hours. After Marcy was born, the long hours started to bother me because I now had to split my time at home between two children. This didn't leave me much time with either one.

Faith: A year and a half after Marcy was born, we

had our third child, Jonas. At this point, I began to get a little restless with the job I was in. I was looking for a more challenging position and found part-time work in a hospital emergency room. I was not looking for full-time work right away, but then Jeff started talking about trying to find a job that didn't require so much of his time.

Jeff: I was ready for fewer hours and less stress. Faith found out that full-time work would be available in two months for her, so we sat down to discuss our options. If I could work some on the side, our income would be comparable, if not better, than it currently was, and we would need even less baby-sitting.

Faith: As we were discussing it, we realized that we would have more family time together and that pretty much clinched the decision for us. We made the switch, and I think the results have been good.

Jeff: Yes, I still have stress with caring for three children, but it is much different than the kind of stress I was under before. I find it easier to manage. The extra family time easily makes it worthwhile. For the next five years, until all of the kids are in school, this is what we plan to do. At that point we can reevaluate our options. We both believe that the family time is very important. We decided to have children so we need to take care of them. The next eighteen years of our lives are the child-rearing years. I certainly hope we can do more than just child-rearing, but I think anything beyond that is just a bonus.—**Jeff and Faith Smucker**

3. Maintaining Balance in Volunteer Assignments

We are committed to keeping our individual, marital, and family relationships in balance in the midst of very active lives. This requires making choices about how much we can do outside our family life. A few years ago, we faced one of those times of deciding who's gifts should be used to serve the broader church. Phil was on the General Board of the denomination and Evon was on the Board of Education for the denomination. About the time Phil was asked to serve on the planning committee for the biennial church convention to be held in St. Louis 1999, Evon was asked to serve as the chair for her board. It would have meant even more travel for Phil's already-busy schedule and less time at home with the family. For Evon it would mean more volunteer time on top of her full-time job as a social worker and clinical director.

Because Phil had already served on a number of churchwide committees, he felt Evon should have an opportunity to chair her board. They believed that if both continued on volunteer assignments, it would keep them from fulfilling their family priorities. Travel and e-mail from both volunteer roles, on top of their jobs, were already impacting family schedules and throwing relationships out of balance. So Phil resigned from the General Board. We believe it was a positive decision. We built a freedom fence we feel good about!—**Phil and Evon Bergey**

4. Athletics and Teen Priorities

Our son Brandon was struggling with the newfound success of being a young high school student who had a head start in several key areas. He had matured physically very early and was often mistaken for an older student. Because of his strength and speed, he made varsity soccer as a freshman. He developed relationships with juniors and seniors. For these reasons, his first two high school years were greatly accelerated. Things were going a little too quickly, and Brandon began losing perspective. He began taking things for granted. He assumed everything went like this in life. Never a bad kid, Brandon began drifting away from God.

During the winter and spring of Brandon's sophomore year, through two separate sporting incidents, he completely tore the main ligament in his right knee. Brandon needed surgery and a six-month recovery with extensive rehabilitation. Suddenly Brandon was confronted with his dependency on medical professionals, on his parents, and on God.

On the day he turned sixteen, instead of being able to drive a car, Brandon was relying on his parents to help him get dressed or to go to the bathroom. Lying around waiting for small improvements like being able to bend his leg without intense pain, Brandon gained a new perspective on life. He began to realize how much he had to be thankful for.

Phil and Evon had the opportunity to either complain about Brandon's adolescence or to find ways to challenge Brandon to see the long view. During Brandon's recovery, Phil took Brandon with him on a trip to Mexico City to visit churches in a sister conference. Despite the injury, Brandon hobbled around Mexico with a cane.

Instead of being bitter, the experience allowed Brandon and his parents to put their relationships in perspective again. Most importantly, this injury allowed Brandon to realize his own dependency on God's love and God's healing touch. Brandon sealed the decision to follow Christ, which he had made several years earlier, and chose to be baptized during the early part of his recovery. This freedom fence experience allowed Brandon to see and appreciate God in new ways and to order his life according to God's purposes, not his own.—**Phil and Evon Bergey**

5. Friendships Outside of Marriage

A single woman was a teacher and a coach at a private middle school. She was a Christian and highly regarded by her peers and students. She developed a special bond with a student and eventually with the student's parents. The parents helped out with fund-raisers and extra projects. The teacher and the parents enjoyed one another's company. One time the teacher asked the father of the student to drive one of the buses for an away game. He was happy to help out. After the kids were taken home, the teacher and the student's father stopped at a restaurant for a cup of coffee. The teacher thought nothing of this spontaneous interaction.

Partway through the cup of coffee, the father of her student said calmly, "I know this happened innocently, but I am now struggling a bit with some feelings for you that make me uncomfortable. I cannot ever do this again. I love my wife and kids, and I respect you. Therefore I cannot put myself in a situation which may lead me to harm the people I care about the most."

It took the teacher by complete surprise. She thought they were just stopping off for coffee. When did the thoughts of an improper relationship come in? She was thankful that the man was frank, and she was happy to respect his wishes. She had certainly not meant any harm. Both now are happy that they built a fence when the freedom felt risky!

6. Children and Church Camp

When I was ten years old, I went to a Christian camp. Besides the mice in our cabins, bland food, and a few rainy afternoons, the experience provided many fun times: games, swimming, crafts, hikes, new friends. Nothing prepared me for the last night at camp. All the campers and counselors went to a campfire worship time deep in the woods on a dark night. We sang. A few counselors shared their testimonies. Then a visiting evangelist began to preach. He used images and words of hell that evoked terror in my soul. I had never heard about such an angry God before. He said that if we wanted to be saved, we could stay and accept Jesus. If we were not ready to be saved, we could walk back to our cabins.

What ten-year-old child could even consider leaving? It was pitch black beyond the reaches of the campfire. I think every child accepted Jesus that night! It stung and bewildered me. I remember returning home and flopping down on the kitchen floor. Mom sat on the floor beside me and listened while I described this perplexing event. She assured me that Jesus did want me to follow him, but out of love, not fear. The fence that was built by that preacher was extremely narrow and unwelcoming.

When I was fourteen years old, I took another chance and went to a different church camp. It was a frenzy of fun and new friendships. This camp staff also planned times of worship. We sang. Counselors shared their testimonies. We learned about a God of love and a Christ of compassion. On a rainy evening, we crowded into a meeting room to worship. An invitation was given for us to become followers of Jesus, and many of us enthusiastically accepted this call. The fence this camp used was wide and welcoming. I returned home warmed by this commitment. I give thanks for the freedom and the invitation the camp leaders gave me to follow Christ.

7. Stay-at-Home Mom

I am a parent of three precious little girls, ages seven, five, and two. I am a full-time, stay-at-home mother, which I love and at times hate. But I believe and know that the job of parenting that I am doing is an awesomely important task. To think that I play a major role in forming their images of God, their feelings about themselves and the world around them humbles and at times scares me. What an awesome responsibility! Their images of God as their parent will be directly reflected in the parent that I have been to them. I show love and acceptance toward them and the closeness that we develop will be the reference point from which they will view God and his love for them.

Parenting can be a frustrating job. I've heard it said that there are two kinds of people: BE-ers and DO-ers. I don't believe that I am an extreme in this but I would say that I am a DO-er. When I don't or can't get measurable things accomplished, I get frustrated. With three young children, I find it very difficult to get many things checked off my daily list. Frequently I find myself interrupted mid-sentence with a cry for "Mom," when I am trying to answer a question or solve a problem for one of my other children.

But throughout the day, while I am frantically working so hard and seemingly accomplishing so little, more is taking place than meets the eye. Lots of learning is happening whether I am aware of it or not, through my words and, more importantly, through the way I deal with them and the situations that we encounter during the day. They are constantly learning about honesty, integrity, communication, and relationships among many other things.

Kids can ask some pretty hard questions. Jenna, my seven-year-old, asked me yesterday, "Mom, why are we here on the earth?" These are the times when parenting scares me. I found myself very hesitant to answer. How am I equipped to answer such a philosophical question?

I was a biology student in college!

But these are important questions and ones that provide an opportunity to further share my faith in God and his plan for us and the world. I answered in a way that let her know that I believe God has made us to please and honor him. But also in a way that will hopefully keep her asking this and many other questions throughout her life.

Although parenting is a difficult and sometimes thankless job, there are many rewards. The intimacy and trust that a child gives to a parent, the warmth of a hug, the need for your kiss before being tucked into bed at night, the secrets shared, and the comfort that only a parent can give makes the job well worth the toil. We as parents are helping to shape other lives. This indeed is sacred work.—**Joyce Longenecker**

8. Facing Limits on Careers

Nora and Curt both have professional careers. Prior to having children, both worked full-time. Their careers were their main focus: schooling, internships, and talking through cases. After their first child was born, their careers began to change in stages. At first, Nora worked part-time while Curt began a new job and part-time graduate school. Then with the addition of a second child, Nora decided to be at home full-time. When Curt finished with school, he made a decision to drastically reduce the time and energy that was needed at the beginning of his career. He and Nora are now focusing on their family life together.

They have made a deliberate choice for Curt to be the income provider and for Nora to be primary child-care parent and home manager. Curt has a job that he likes because it is extremely conducive to family life. No evenings, no weekends, and minimal stress most days.

It provides outstanding benefits for the family too: vacation time, insurance, close to doctor's office that allows him to be at the children's appointments.

Curt doesn't "love" his job, but he loves his life. The emphasis on career can change later when the children are through high school. He is satisfied with the balance. Even though he has had opportunities for advancement, Curt and Nora decided he should turn them down because of the cost of the added responsibilities, increase in hours, and the stresses that advancement could bring to the family. The increase in income could not replace family time and the intimate relationship he has with Nora and his children.

Nora has come to peace with taking a leave from her professional career. Knowing that she has at least twenty-five years to work after the children are older makes the small picture more focused. Seeing the children more settled with a more predictable schedule and slower pace is very gratifying. Also, she has more opportunity to be supported as a mother now that she has time to attend a church program for mothers in her neighborhood. She also gets together with other mothers and their children informally.

9. Freeing Elderly Parents

"If I ever move from this house, I will have to be carried out." These words echoed in our ears many times as my parents entered their eighties and we suggested they think about putting their names on a list to enter a retirement home. My two siblings were living out of state, so the care of my aging parents fell on me and my wife. Throughout his life, my father was very capable of making his own decisions, often without consulting other members of the family. So we knew for him to move from this house that he lived in for over sixty years would have to be his decision.

As it turned out, Mother's health deteriorated to the point that she need to be moved to a nursing care facility. My father continued to live at home and visited Mother daily. But life at home became very lonely, as his church, family, and friends were unable to give him the support that he needed. And so six months after Mother moved out of the house, he made the decision to move to the retirement home to be near her. We felt good about his decision.

My wife and I were always available for my father, allowing him to be independent as much and as long as possible. At one point, we realized that he should no longer be driving. With the help of his doctor, the state did not renew his driver's license. The reality of not driving was very hard for him to accept, and we made ourselves available to chauffeur him to wherever he needed to go.

As his health deteriorated, he no longer felt comfortable or secure in his room in independent living. He needed the assurance that a nurse would be readily available if needed. We suggested that he move to assisted living. Eventually, when he was ready, he made the decision to move! He always seemed to know when the time was right to make significant changes. About two weeks after he make that move, he passed away at the age of ninety.

Even though my wife and I needed to give a lot of time to my parents in their final years, we are happy now that we did. We were able to talk many things over with them and to clear some things up, especially with my father. With the help of a counselor, we were able to talk with him about his approaching death and even planned for his funeral with him. We felt freed up by the openness. When he died we were at peace.—**Glenn and Anne Weaver**

10. Consecutive Versus Concurrent Careers

Life is one's story woven in cycles. Each story is unique and reflects the choices one makes in each cycle. In my current cycle, I am preparing to return to school for my fourteenth year in teaching first grade. My colleagues are all younger than I am. In fact, some of them are younger than my children. But why is it that I have lots of energy and they are tired in the mornings, exhausted in the afternoon, and use the word "stress" a lot? They have bought into the illusion of the American dream that happiness is graduating from college, getting married, getting a good job, buying a big house, and preferably in that order! After a couple of years on the job, they begin their families.

Most of them come back to work in less than a year, and some are back in a few months. I console and listen to mothers who come to work crying because they had to leave their babies at daycare or with Grandmas and they want to be at home with their babies. They say they have to work to maintain the lifestyle they chose before they had children. They are frustrated because they feel torn between the two worlds. They realize that they are not able to give their best at school or at home. I often hear, "I'm not a good mother, and I'm not a good teacher anymore." They are already tired when they come to school after being up at night with sick children.

When I graduated from college thirty-four years ago, I taught and studied for several years, here and then abroad with a church relief and service agency. When our first child was born, I chose to stay at home with him. Five years later, I continued at home with a second child. The choice to be at home meant that we lived a very simple lifestyle. However, when Mom doesn't go off to work, there is no childcare to pay, fewer clothes are needed, and there is more time to prepare food. There was time for friends and for play groups. I did part-time tutoring when the children were in elementary school. This was ideal because I could see them off to school and be home when they returned.

This cycle of motherhood, with a break from career, lasted until my younger child started junior high school. The shift to full-time career was an adjustment for all of us. Supper waiting on the table was no longer the norm. We began juggling household chores and time together as a family was more difficult to arrange. I have always been grateful that I chose to have prime time with my children. And now, I find I have renewed energy to give to my first graders. While most teachers my age are retiring and are burned out from teaching thirty years, I wonder if I'll ever be ready to retire!

11. Boundary Making for Children

Lane is a little three-year-old boy with a large amount of energy. He has blond hair and sparkling eyes. He is a favorite of everyone who meets him. He can steal your heart with his smile or bring you to tears with his love of mischief. As a busy mother of three preschoolers, I am constantly looking for ways to keep my energetic son out of trouble. Since having the freedom to roam the entire house at will inevitably results in catastrophe, our family has adopted a special activity for Lane known as mat time.

After my baby girl is tucked in for her morning nap and my five-year-old has started his kindergarten work, a mat is spread on the floor. The location is within close proximity of my daily work, and soon a happy little Lane is busily playing with Legos on his mat. For thirty to forty-five minutes, peace and order will reign in our home.

Lane enjoys the boundary of mat time. It helps him develop self-control, concentration, and creativity by focusing his boundless energy on just one or two toys. Without mat time, the sky is the limit for this child.

We have found it to be a wonderful tool in our family.—**Teresa Weaver**

12. Parent Hobbies That Benefit the Family

There are crossroads moments that help to define who we are. I had such a moment when a friend and I went to the Philadelphia Guitar Show. What I did not know before I went to the guitar show was that an adjoining area of the convention hall was occupied by the Philadelphia Gun Show, my former beloved hobby. As I entered the lobby, I found myself being drawn into the gun show to just look around. Thousands of guns stacked upon one another. Mostly men were adoring these guns. They were sighting down the barrels and checking the actions. The sights and smells were old familiar friends to me. Memories flooded back to me of the hunting trips with my father and friends.

My thoughts were interrupted by my two-year-old daughter saying, "Let's go, Daddy, let's go!" At that moment, I knew why I had laid that hobby to rest. Why I had recently traded my guns for guitars. Guns took me away from my family. Guitar playing brought me back home. Because I am the income provider at this stage of our family life, I am already gone from home forty hours a week. Hunting took me away for additional days. I missed my family, and they missed me. I ultimately had to ask myself how my goals of family life matched up with my hobby life.

It took awhile for me to bury a hobby that had meant so much to me. I know in my heart it was not a compatible arrangement. One Friday afternoon, I asked my father-in-law to go with me to sell my guns at a sporting goods store. I had come this far; I did not want to change my mind. There was a great release in knowing that I had made a necessary and willing sacrifice for my own good and the well-being of our family.

Two years earlier my spouse, Anne, had bought me a guitar and arranged for lessons. Guitar playing grew on me. It met a huge need. Playing guitar is a stress reliever from a busy day. It is an opportunity for worship. It provides entertainment and learning opportunities for our children. Anne and I sit on the deck and sing together after the children are in bed. If the children are having a hard time falling asleep, I play the guitar softly until they drift off to sleep. I play in church or Sunday school as often as I can.

I could not have found a hobby that has given more life to our family. Neither could I have found a hobby that gives me the escape from a demanding profession that guitar playing does. Hardly a day goes by without playing one of my Martin guitars. I have found freedom! Martin Luther King said, "Let freedom ring!" I say, "Let freedom strum!"—**Todd Weaver**

13. Parental Involvement in the Child's Education

We have three children, ages eleven, nine, and five. Our oldest son began sixth grade in middle school. He received good grades in elementary school. When he began sixth grade, his activities were soccer, violin, drums in the band, and orchestra. Middle school was difficult. Adjusting to the new schedule of changing teachers and classrooms throughout the day was a burden. His grades began slipping very quickly.

My husband and I met with his teachers and guidance counselor to figure out what was happening and to work together to find a positive solution. We agreed that our son would have an assignment sheet signed each day by his homeroom teacher, and then when he completed the assignments, by us. His grades immediately went back up, and he was more satisfied with his school performance. If he would slack off, there were consequences in place. He could not wear his favorite jeans for one week! This would quickly remedy the problem, and he would get back on track.

It became clear that he had a hard time keeping up with all of the changes at middle school and needed more structure. He knew what our expectations were, and we were quick to be proactive for him. We have begun talking with our son about a plan for seventh grade. He is not sure how much help he will need so we will give him a chance to keep track of his homework on his own. We are prepared to meet with the teachers and guidance counselors again if necessary. We want to give our son the necessary structure but also want him to develop some on his own.

14. Children and Organized Sports

Daryl has been a soccer coach for seventeen years and played organized soccer for nine years (including college). Audrey also was an athlete, having played field hockey for eight years. They have four children, ages fourteen, twelve, ten, and six. Daryl and Audrey have made deliberate decisions regarding their children's participation in sports. While they see the importance of organized sports, they also believe that the involvement needs to be controlled for the good of the children and family life. They do not let their children join a team before they are ten years old and do not permit them to play on junior high school teams. They believe that children need time for themselves, especially during the school year. They guide child-directed play at home, including four-square, exercising on the trampoline, and other activities.

They are convinced that the emphasis on competition, comparison with less talented team members, and the pursuit of scholarships are harmful to children. Parents can be misled if they think that starting their child in sports at a young age will lead to success. Many burn out by the time they are in high school, lose out on other important parts of their childhood, and very few receive athletic scholarships. While Daryl and Audrey support their children who are in sports, they do not attend all of their games, and the family is not centered on competitive athletics. They believe that a well-balanced family is more important. The fences they have put around sports give them freedom.—**From an interview with Daryl and Audrey Groff**

15. Freed Through Sacrifice

I was born into the home of a preacher and throughout the years have been blessed with many other preachers in my life, including an uncle who was a missionary, a brother, eight cousins, a son, a lay preacher son, a grandson-in-law, and a great grandson. The surviving members of my family are still actively serving the church. With all these preachers around, I can hear people say, "She should be able to memorize the Bible from beginning to end after being subjected to all that theology from birth."

Because my father was an evangelist who traveled throughout the United States and Canada, he acquired many acquaintances. Numerous people who heard him preach were very eager to visit our home. We lived in a very large house. We had a number of beds that were always ready for expected or unexpected visitors, much to the dismay of my sister and me. This was before the days of automatic washers and dryers and wash-and-wear materials. Every piece of linen had to be meticulously ironed before other visitors used the beds. We were irritated at times when this procedure had to be repeated. But we will never know—could we have been entertaining angels unawares?

Did we feel hemmed in by having to cancel some preplanned enjoyable entertainment for that particular evening? Perhaps. I must confess it wasn't always done in the spirit of love, but we were rewarded by enlarging our circle of friends throughout the United States, Canada, India, South America, and the Ukraine. Rather than feel resentful, I have enlarged my vision and love for my beloved church and gained many long-time friends through this sacrifice. Besides, because of my father's calling as an evangelist, our family learned to appreciate travel. When I was still a young girl in the early part of this century, we went to the West Coast by train. That love of travel continues to bless my whole family. No, I am not resentful. The few sacrifices I made gave me a larger view of life.—**Margaret Kaufman**

16. Family Traditions

I grew up in a family where special practices were an important part of holidays. When I married, I felt that my spouse and I needed to continue similar patterns that had been part of my family's experience. This got complicated, especially when children entered the picture and we had two family backgrounds to take into consideration. Eventually the realization came that in order for me to separate from my family of origin and develop a closeness and identity with my "new" family, we needed to develop our own special traditions.

Developing these traditions has been fun and has

evolved naturally. Mealtimes in themselves can be important family traditions, and we find that many of our special times involve food.

+Every Sunday morning (even on vacation when possible) my husband makes baked oatmeal for breakfast.

+On the first day of school, the children choose a restaurant at which to celebrate.

+When a child has a birthday, my husband takes her out alone for breakfast.

+Each fall before the start of school, I take each child school shopping alone, concluding with supper at a restaurant the child chooses. This has become a special mother and daughter event.

+We have a whole set of rituals surrounding the Christmas season. These include Advent routines, going to a Chinese restaurant on Christmas Eve, David's Christmas bread, the order of gift opening, and the Christmas dinner menu.

I realize how important these traditions have become to my daughters. When the various situations approach, they are quick to remind me and to make plans. Hopefully these small events will continue to strengthen the bonds of our family life. We believe that.—**Rachel Martin**

17. Enough

Did I do enough for her?
We jumped in puddles and licked
chocolate beaters.
We face painted and cut up magazines.
We went to parks, we hid from dogs.
We read and read and read.

We had boring, useless hours,
Barney one too many times,
Tears and time outs,
Anger and apologies.
We counted the minutes until Todd came home.

We raised each other.
"You can't always have what you want
when you want it."
"There are times to be persistent
and times to be patient."
"There are three children to take
care of here."
"Take a deep breath, relax."
"You can solve this problem peacefully."

Did I do enough for my daughter?
"Mom, a boy cried at school."
"Mom, I told my stomach not
to be sick today."
"Mom, a boy said he'd kick my
butt if I did not draw a skeleton.
I told the teacher and she
gave him time out."

You lessen my fears, daughter, you
    lessen my fears.
But you cannot take me to the hamster
    cage.
  You cannot make my sick stomach
    go away.
  You cannot protect me from
    stories about bullies.
I will pray, my child, that God will be
    enough for both mother and daughter.

—*Anne Kaufman Weaver*

Activity

What are your freedom stories? Share them with others!

The authors

Gerald and Marlene Kaufman

Anne Kaufman Weaver and Nina Kaufman Harnish

Gerald W. Kaufman, LSW, ACSW, BCD, received an undergraduate degree from Goshen (Ind.) College and a masters in social work from Indiana University.

Gerald has been in private practice since 1974. Prior to that he served as adjunct professor at Elizabethtown (Pa.) College and Harrisburg (Pa.) Area Community College. He also served as chief social worker at Philhaven Hospital, Lebanon, Pa., and in the department of Psychiatry at Penn State School of Medicine, Hershey, Pa.

L. Marlene Kaufman, LSW, received an undergraduate degree from Goshen (Ind.) College and a masters in social work from Temple University, Philadelphia, Pa.

Marlene and Gerald founded Kaufman Counseling Service in Akron, Pa., in 1980. In their practice they counsel individuals, families, and couples.

Both are members of the Akron (Pa.) Mennonite Church. Gerald has served as congregational chairman, and Marlene served as an elder on the pastoral team.

Together they have led numerous classes and seminars locally as well as in other areas of the church across North America.

Gerald grew up in Johnstown, Pa., and Marlene in Gibson City, Ill. They now live in Akron, Pa. Four married children and eight grandchildren are part of their household.

Anne Kaufman Weaver, MSW, received her undergraduate degree from Eastern Mennonite University, Harrisonburg, Va., and her masters in social work from Marywood College, Scranton, Pa. She also completed one year of study in the School of Spiritual Formation, Wernersville, Pa.

Anne has worked as a case manager for the homebound elderly in northwest Philadelphia and as youth pastor at Blooming Glen (Pa.) Mennonite Church. Presently she is a stay-at-home mother. She is a member at Blooming Glen Mennonite Church and currently serves on the board of elders. Anne was born in Michigan City, Ind. She is married to Todd Weaver, DMD. They live in Telford, Pa., with their three children.

Nina Kaufman Harnish, RD. Nina received her degree from Goshen (Ind.) College and did her internship in dietetics at University of Virginia Hospital.

Nina has worked in public health settings and has done individual and group counseling classes as a registered dietitian. She is presently a stay-at-home mom. Nina was born in Lebanon, Pa. She is married to Craig Harnish, MSW. They live in Leola, Pa., with their two sons. They are members at Akron Mennonite Church. Nina has served as elder on the pastoral team and is presently chair of the children's ministry team.